THE CAPACITY TO

Wendy Hollway explores a subject that is largely absent from the topical literature on care. Humans are not born with a capacity to care, and this volume explores how this capacity is achieved through the experiences of primary care, gender development and later, parenting.

In this book, the author addresses the assumption that the capacity to care is innate. She argues that key processes in the early development of babies and young children create the capability for individuals to care, with a focus on the role of intersubjective experience and parent–child relations. *The Capacity to Care* also explores the controversial belief that women are better at caring than men and questions whether this is likely to change with contemporary shifts in parenting and gender relations. Similarly, the sensitive domain of the quality of care and how to consider whether care has broken down are also debated, alongside a consideration of what constitutes a 'good enough' family.

The Capacity to Care provides a unique theorization of the nature of selfhood, drawing on developmental and object relations psychoanalysis, philosophical and feminist literatures. It will be of relevance to social scientists studying gender development, gender relations and the family as well as those interested in the ethics of care debate.

WOMEN AND PSYCHOLOGY
Series Editor: Jane Ussher
School of Psychology,
University of Western Sydney

This series brings together current theory and research on women and psychology. Drawing on scholarship from a number of different areas of psychology, it bridges the gap between abstract research and the reality of women's lives by integrating theory and practice, research and policy.

Each book addresses a 'cutting edge' issue of research, covering such topics as post-natal depression, eating disorders, theories and methodologies.

The series provides accessible and concise accounts of key issues in the study of women and psychology, and clearly demonstrates the centrality of psychology to debates within women's studies or feminism.

The Series Editor would be pleased to discuss proposals for new books in the series.

Other titles in this series:

THE THIN WOMAN
Helen Malson

THE MENSTRUAL CYCLE
Anne E. Walker

POST-NATAL DEPRESSION
Paula Nicolson

RE-THINKING ABORTION
Mary Boyle

WOMEN AND AGING
Linda R. Gannon

BEING MARRIED. DOING GENDER
Caroline Dryden

UNDERSTANDING DEPRESSION
Janet M. Stoppard

FEMININITY AND THE PHYSICALLY ACTIVE WOMAN
Precilla Y.L. Choi

GENDER, LANGUAGE AND DISCOURSE
Anne Weatherall

THE SCIENCE/FICTION OF SEX
Annie Potts

THE PSYCHOLOGICAL DEVELOPMENT OF GIRLS AND WOMEN
Sheila Greene

JUST SEX?
Nicola Gavey

WOMAN'S RELATIONSHIP WITH HERSELF
Helen O'Grady

GENDER TALK
Susan A. Speer

BEAUTY AND MISOGYNY
Sheila Jeffreys

BODY WORK
Sylvia K. Blood

MANAGING THE MONSTROUS FEMININE
Jane M. Ussher

THE CAPACITY TO CARE

Gender and Ethical Subjectivity

Wendy Hollway

Routledge
Taylor & Francis Group

LONDON AND NEW YORK

First published 2006
by Routledge
27 Church Road, Hove, East Sussex BN3 2FA

Simultaneously published in the USA and Canada
by Routledge
270 Madison Avenue, New York, NY 10016

Routledge is an imprint of the Taylor & Francis Group, an informa business

© 2006 Psychology Press

Typeset in Times New Roman by
Keystroke, 28 High Street, Tettenhall, Wolverhampton
Printed and bound in Great Britain by
T J International Ltd, Padstow, Cornwall
Paperback cover design by Anú Design

British Library Cataloguing in Publication Data
A catalogue record for this book is available from the British Library

Library of Congress Cataloging in Publication Data
Hollway, Wendy.
The capacity to care : gender and ethical subjectivity /
Wendy Hollway.
p. cm. – (Women and psychology)
Includes bibliographical references and index.
ISBN 0–415–39967-X (hardback) – ISBN 0–415–39968–8 (pbk.)
1. Caring. 2. Women–Psychology. I. Title. II. Series.
BJ1475.H66 2006
155.2′32–dc22
2006015101

ISBN 13: 978–0-415–39967–8 (hbk)
ISBN 13: 978–0-415–39968–5 (pbk)
ISBN 10: 0–415–39967-X (hbk)
ISBN 10: 0–415–39968–8 (pbk)

CONTENTS

ACKNOWLEDGEMENTS

A remarkable number of people have supported me in the preparation of this book. First and foremost, thanks go to my brother Roger and his wife Jan with whom I stayed in Auckland, New Zealand during the months in which I wrote the first draft. It was home from home in the true sense; that I felt I could relax, be myself and do what I needed to do. Second, thanks go to the readers, from a wide range of disciplinary backgrounds, who commented on the draft or ideas that went into it: Lisa Baraitser, Ben Bradley, Andrew Dobson, Heather Elliott, Brid Featherstone, Lynn Froggett, Stephen Frosh, David Gadd, Tony Jefferson, Ann Phoenix, Peter Redman, Sasha Roseneil, Jane Selby, Selma Sevenhuijsen, Elizabeth Silva, Cathy Urwin, Margaret Wetherell, Fiona Williams. They helped me extend my intellectual reach across several disciplinary areas. I want also to thank the Faculty of Social Sciences at the Open University, which in the past five years has provided me with support, recognition, intellectual stimulation and friendship: care that I am fortunate to experience from a workplace. Finally, without my family's capacities to care, what I have written in this book would have been unthinkable.

DEDICATION
TO ELLA AND TONY

1

INTRODUCING THE CAPACITY TO CARE

Approaches to care

What is the capacity to care and why does it matter? How is it acquired? What are its origins in the early development of self and morality? Are women better at caring than men and, if so, is this likely to change with contemporary changes in parenting and gender relations? What would constitute a good-enough family, as opposed to good-enough mothering? How does the capacity to care inform the ethics of care debate about relationality and autonomy and their gender? How do people care across distance and difference? These are the questions that are addressed in this book. Through them I attempt to provide the current social discourses with an adequate psychology as a resource for understanding care, in the domains of theory, policy and practice.

During the week in which I finalised this manuscript, The *Observer* Sunday newspaper (26 March 2006) had a two-page spread on women who are 'young successful, well-paid', asking 'are they killing feminism?'. It was based on a magazine article by a British academic, Alison Wolf, who argues that this manifestation of young womanhood 'has dire consequences for society', one of which is that the pursuit of certain careers (a successful young woman investment banker is profiled) is turning women away from caring, in the form of both having children and entering the caring professions. According to Wolf, we are seeing 'the end of female altruism'.

In this and many similar ways, the principal theme of this book – the gender of the capacity to care and ethical subjectivity – is central to contemporary public debate. This debate, including the overdrawn claims and ill-conceived arguments, is symptomatic of the profound anxieties that continue to accompany changes in gender relations in the new millennium. I hope that I succeed in my attempt to provide an analysis that is not hijacked by those anxieties – which can lead either to amplifying or denying the problems and potential of changing gender relations for care. 'Society' has indeed in many ways depended on women to care, and on their 'female altruism' to motivate their ongoing capacity to care. As the realignment of caring is precipitated by the tectonic plate tremors of gender differences, it is a challenge to ensure that everyone has access to good-enough care, not only infants, children, the old, sick and disadvantaged but also so-called independent adults and

1

the carers themselves. Can both women and men access capacities to care freed up by the relaxation of rigid gender binaries? Through conceptualising some universal aspects of self – aspects that go beyond gender as well as those enabled and suppressed by particular gender regimes – I envisage ways that women and men can tap into the identificatory potential of every human being who relates to others through both their individuality and their intersubjectivity.

Why is it important to understand the capacity to care, as well as focusing on the resources and practices concerning care? When individuals fail to care for those they encounter, those others suffer. But that is just the start. The effect is not just suffering (which ameliorates) but psychological trauma. If, as I argue, people are relational in the core of their being, then systematic and continuous failures of care have profound impact on a person's character and how they relate to others. This then creates a ripple effect in the social relations around each such person: care-less and hate-ful individuals are hard to care for and this has effects on the would-be carer as well as on the person in need of care. When whole groups fail to care, cultures of hate, retribution and vengeance can be created that reproduce the traumatic conditions of their own making. There is less chance of the kind of citizenly care that provides a bulwark against political corruption, unbridled market forces or religious fundamentalism. Moreover, there is created an intergenerational dynamic that is harder to interrupt by social and political interventions when harmful individuals are drawn to reproduce the conditions of their own psychological damage. A convincing test of such an assertion is to look into the biography of any violent criminal, serial killer or psychopathic aggressor. They have invariably suffered deprivation, not necessarily of material resources but of relationships characterised by trust, safety, respect and love. These are enabled by the capacity to care of significant others around them.[1]

A psycho-social inquiry does not therefore reduce to individual or interpersonal problems but underpins the big questions of society, politics, ethics and global environmental sustainability. Although I start my inquiry by asking how the capacity to care is first established in the intimate relations of care between maternal figures and infants, by the end of the book I have broadened it out to explore how the capacity to care is implicated in institutional change and caring about strangers across difference and distance. Hardly a day goes by without these issues featuring in the news. In the same week as the newspaper feature about 'the end of female altruism', the Archbishop of Canterbury was interviewed on the morning radio news. He talked about the political failure to address global warming and its ethical implications, namely that because of western people's energy consumption, populations in the developing world would be dramatically destabilised and billions would probably die. On the same evening, two television documentaries showed the particularity of people suffering through political and institutional failures to care; the first was about African economic migrants trying to enter Europe illegally, the second about the underfunding of care for the elderly in the UK, told by the son of an old woman suffering from dementia, as he examined his conscience about putting her in a 'care home', rather than caring for her at home.

Many writers concerned with the state of the world, from philosophy to political and social theory, have converged on the question of living with difference (for example, Arendt 1958, Levinas 1985/1999, Mouffe 2000, Connolly 2002). Ideal arrangements or attitudes are discussed in order to imagine ethical connections among people in the public sphere who are different from each other. However, few of these writers ask how – psychologically – respect for difference and care across difference are achieved. I am critical of any paradigm that does not appreciate how psychic structures and processes transform and co-construct experience and culturally dominant forms of living. My aim is to supplement overly social and exclusively abstract paradigms of ethics, morality and care by providing a dynamic psychological account, situated in the relevant social contexts and anchored in life historical time. This produces an approach in which I ask, for example, how the capacity to care across difference is nurtured, from what starting points. The result is a rare focus on the effects of life histories of being cared for and caring; the vicissitudes of self development that are crucial in a person's later capacity for care across difference.

This is also an unpopular perspective: recent social science has rejected the paradigm of psychological development and focused on situating people in the present. It has also largely rejected the trope of the family, seeing it as a conservative sphere in which difference is defended against. My argument is that certain conditions that start early in life within families (families of all types) are usually decisive for later psychological capacities that produce caring (or hostile) relations to difference in others. These capacities may begin in families but they do not need to end there. Every person's life history is contained in their internal world and this internal world is active in shaping the ways the person encounters current, everyday events and relationships, including the challenge of caring for familiars and strangers.

Care is a broad term, which perhaps should be broken down into narrower categories, but the fact that the word has come to cover such a broad and varied remit is significant in itself and I shall try to work with the penumbra of meanings to which it gives rise rather than shoehorn these into tidy categories. There is a huge literature on care, but there is a startling absence on the subject of capacity to care in theory, and of research and writing on care. The care literature mainly takes two forms. First there is a philosophical literature, which includes a substantial body of work on ethics discussed at an abstract level. Second are the social work and social policy literatures, which tend to be directed towards advocacy for carers and working out the best arrangements, supports and resources to enable caring, paid and unpaid, to take place. More recently, this has included an empirically focused literature with both theoretical and policy orientations. Williams (2004), reporting the conclusions of a large, empirically based research programme that brings together many of these strands, argues for an ethic of care that extends from private into political domains and recognises the importance of care ethics in people's lives and how these can be carried out in a diversity of living arrangements and family groups.

Because of women's historical association with caring, feminist literatures have been prolific and these have reflected the same two emphases, the first taking the shape of an extended debate about the ethics of care and its relation to gender, and the second looking at caring as an activity. Managing the juggling act between paid employment and care is, understandably, a recurring theme in the latter. Both are often premised on understanding care in the light of women's subordination; often on the position that caring is associated with women's oppression and reproduces it.

These different tracks often reflect what has become quite a well-established conceptual distinction between caring about and caring for (Fisher and Tronto 1990, Skeggs 1997, Sevenhuijsen 1998):

> Caring about which involves social dispositions that operate at a personal level and assume a relationship between the carer and cared for, and caring for which involves the actual practice of caring, involving specific tasks such as lifting, cleaning and cooking, and does not necessarily relate to caring about.
>
> (Skeggs 1997: 67)

My interest is about the psychological capacities involved in care, and this book therefore emphasises caring about: the term 'capacity to care' addresses questions to do with caring about. The disadvantage of the phrase 'capacity to care' is its connotation of a singular, static entity, whereas I address something dynamic, variable and situated; ideas perhaps better captured by the term 'caring about'. However, I wish to retain the connotation of relative consistency associated with the idea of core capacity as a result of its early roots, which, although they can be modified, cannot be overridden by rational decision. Moreover, caring about and caring for are not as separable as Skeggs' neat definitions imply, because in my framework, the practices of care and their meanings are part of a series of mutually affecting dynamics that have an impact on caring about, which likewise affects practices. Caring about occurs in the context of practices and relations involving caring for. For Lynn Froggett, 'Both [caring for and caring about] are necessary but it is the latter that lifts caring out of the mire of condescension and abuse of power with which it has sometimes been tainted' (2002: 125). I hope that I shall be able to convey what the qualities of caring about involve if they are to achieve this not inconsiderable feat.

Once I started reading the care literatures with a question in mind about the capacity to care, I noticed that they were often based on an unexamined assumption, namely that, given the appropriate resources and supports, people will care adequately. Of course, given the long history of belief that women are natural carers, it is not surprising that the assumption continues that women want, and know how, to care. I hope that a sustained focus on the capacity to care can further expose the residues of this assumption, which remains despite the fact that the natural ability of women to care has been profoundly called into question, both ideologically and empirically. What is more, women's identities and roles are changing within changing gender relations. Where the care of children is concerned, the assumption of an unproblematic capacity to care now often includes fathers as well as mothers, as we can see in the shift to the term 'parenting' where 'mothering' used to be the common term. In describing and theorising the vicissitudes of acquiring the capacities involved in caring, I want first to problematise the assumption that the capacity to care is natural, which has led to it being taken for granted, and second to challenge the notion that it is simply social, the result of habit, training or practice.

Babies are not born with capacities to care and the acquisition of the morality that underpins good caring is a complex and conflictual process that is an integral part of psychological development. Boys and girls experience the development of identity in very different ways because of the deeply entrenched meanings of gender everywhere around them. The meanings of care are gendered too and so the acquisition of the capacities associated with caring is never a gender-neutral process. So, throughout this book my account keeps in mind the gendering of the capacity to care. It sets this question in the contemporary context of seismic changes in gender relations (in Western cultures in particular) in order to be able to explore what are likely to be their effects on women's and men's capacities to care.

I do not subscribe to assumptions about care being the natural capacity of women. However, social science has been afflicted by the kind of binary thinking that argues that if it is not natural it must be social. Post-structuralist feminist accounts have evolved out of the political imperative to challenge arguments based on women's biology and also out of a trenchant critique of views of subjectivity that assumed a pre-given, unitary and rational (masculine) subject. As a result, however, they commonly risk evacuating subjectivity and ending up with a socially determined subject. This applies even to the more sophisticated treatments of care as in positioning theory.

Beverley Skeggs (1997), for example, is interested in the way that the particular group of working class women that she studied in depth and over time came to construe themselves as caring in the context of the training that they were following. She draws on a Foucauldian idea of subject positions, for example when she inquires into 'the processes by which the caring self is produced through the negotiation and performances of subject positions given by the organisation of the caring courses and caring curricula' (Skeggs 1997: 56). These courses were developed as part of a history of 'many attempts to induce women to enjoy their domestic labour and responsibilities, which Foucault identifies as a form of productive power whereby social regulation can be achieved willingly, even pleasurably, by the participants themselves' (op cit 41). Foucault's account of the production of selves within the circuits of power–knowledge–practice relations is frequently criticised for being deterministic, while being a powerful analysis of the social forces that frame, constrain and produce subjects. Skeggs positions her participants in the range of opportunities and discourses that are available and attempts to splice these together with more psychological considerations, such as the importance of being recognised as 'respectable' in the wider social gaze or her claim that 'the caring subject is constructed by the conflation of caring for with caring about, in which the practices of caring become inseparable from the personal dispositions' (1997: 51). She does not inquire about these personal dispositions. In this book, these dispositions, their origins and trajectories are my primary focus.

Likewise in the more applied literatures, there is a sociological reductionism. Where there is breakdown of care, material and social factors are emphasised as causative: insufficient money and time, competing demands, the low status of caring work, inadequate training and safeguards, women competing with men in the world of work. Perhaps these have been adequate working assumptions. Capacities to care will certainly be put under greater strain if resources and supports are lacking. Where policy is concerned, the greatest help can perhaps be delivered on this terrain (Williams 2004: 73). The longer-term, intergenerational influences on the development of a capacity to care that I shall be focusing on are more likely to elude policy interventions and do not happen within the length of a government's term of office. Uncared for children, growing into anti-social teenagers and perhaps incapable parents themselves, are widespread and the pattern does not straight-forwardly reflect economic circumstances or changes in welfare provision. My question is therefore not just what kind of adult, parental care is good enough to raise happy, well-adjusted children but how this will affect the care that these children are capable of as adults and parents themselves, in families and beyond. The focus of this book is parenting and the care of children because I regard families (in whatever shape and form) as the crucible of subsequent caring relationships.

My analysis is informed by the use of a psycho-social approach; a long-running theme in my work. Broadly, it says that capacities to care are psycho-social in the sense that they develop as part of self development, which is intersubjective, and that the life histories of individuals during the course of this development are inextricably relational and also derive their meaning from their social setting (structures, cultures, practices and discourses). The experience of being cared for is essential in developing the capacity to care. However, one's ongoing experiences of care, and its lack, are profoundly mediated by internal psychological processes. My choice to focus on the capacity to care is a way of providing a psychological account of self to address the absence of a theory of subjectivity in understanding care. However, by taking a psycho-social perspective I avoid falling back into an individualistic account, even while challenging dominant forms of social constructionism.

I draw on a set of psychoanalytic principles that revolve around unconscious conflict in early relational dynamics, starting with mother–child relationships. Take, as an example, the significance for new mothers of having their own mothers around. This should not be reduced to the principle that the mother provides practical child-care support – although it will probably help if she does. Her mother is also central to the meaning of being a mother through that woman's experience of being her mother's child (Chodorow 2002). Her identifications with her mother's care (including its quality) will be expressed in her own mothering practices, which will continue her own course of ethical development, particularised by her contemporary circumstances – her housing, employment, partner status, for example – whose meanings are all influenced by how she grew up and what her home, her parents and their work meant to her. These are, of course, not a copy of her parents' meanings because of generational changes in her world (Brannen *et al.* 2004). As well as always including the social, the psychological capacity to care is also linked to biological characteristics. In my analysis I include the importance of the female, maternal body and the significance of the different reproductive capacities of women and men in early parenting and the effects of these on gendered capacities to care and their likely changes in the twenty-first century.

Because care practices and practising care are not in themselves guarantees of quality, the capacities or dispositions to care need to be addressed. Consequently, this book enters the sensitive terrain of the quality of care. What constitutes good-enough care? There is not one single model for good-quality care and there are probably as many different practices of care as there are contexts, relationships and meanings within which care is exercised. But I shall take the view that there are universal ethical principles too (for example the principle of avoiding violence against others) and consider these alongside the specifics of contemporary Western settings in the idea of capacities to care and how these are expressed in good quality care.

Family conflict and break-up is widely agreed to be influential in children's development, but not all such families produce problem children and not all problem children have experienced conflict among and loss of primary parental figures. What makes the difference? Often, as feminism has regularly pointed out, mothers are blamed for how children turn out, and often they have been the lynchpin of childrearing. Can women's willingness and capacity to care (neither as automatic as the ideology would have us believe) survive changes in gender relations as they are currently manifesting in Britain and other Western countries? The individualisation thesis that is central to current social theory debate argues that the individualisation of late modern societies tends towards self- rather than other-oriented motivations and practices. Is the individualising of women undermining their traditional caring capacities? The newspaper article with which I began this introduction provided an example of this social science debate expressed in popular form.

Individualisation theory provides a literature about social changes impacting on the self that does not assume care to be natural and unalterable. On the contrary, the concept of individualisation refers to the complex processes of social transformation that increasingly produce individuals with a capacity for autonomy, freedom of choice and self reflection, and these processes are assumed to run counter to the affiliations and care obligations that are traditionally rooted in kinship and unequal gender relations in which women put the care of others before their own freedom of choice (Beck and Beck-Gernsheim 1983/2002). They may also run counter to the wishes and needs for dependency, which survive in a conflictual form, jarring with the injunctions of autonomy (Hoggett, 2000). However, this sociological literature does not address changes in the capacity to care, in early or late modernity, perhaps because its exclusive focus on large-scale social transformations leads to an implicit assumption that selves result from these. In contrast, from a psycho-social perspective, I shall emphasise the recalcitrant aspects of selves that make them not so malleable and also render them vulnerable: the anxious, needy, desirous, controlling and above all relational features of self that underpin care. My emphasis on intergenerational transmission suggests that the account of social change in individualisation theory (as in much of social theory) needs modification. Its account of how social change produces changed subjectivity assumes a rapid adjustment to new (individualising) social circumstances. Intergenerational transmission suggests that identifications with an older generation (especially parents and back, through them, with former generations) act as a partial brake on those effects.

The socio-historical perspective of individualisation theory provides an important reminder that contemporary care is subject to a set of normative expectations and resultant pressures that did not exist in previous eras.[2] This is not to accept the view of the degradation of mothering [see Silva (1996) for a detailed critique] but rather to be mindful of its specific conditions and their effects on subjectivity. For example, I consider the ways that daughters and sons differentiate from mothers to be important in the kinds of caring capacities that they later manifest as parents (see Chapter 5). In the case of daughters, the 'need' to differentiate is situated within the late modern, feminist injunction to 'be a subject in one's own right', while at the same time being recognised as having consequences for the capacity to care in contemporary Western cultures.

In search of subjectivity in the literature

I have said that there is a dearth of literatures on the capacity to care. What then are my theoretical starting points? Since Nancy Chodorow's ground-breaking 1978 book, *The reproduction of mothering*,[3] feminist interest in changing women's oppression has included a focus on mothering as a paradigm case of caring, including women's role as mothers in the reproduction of gendered caring in their daughters (see Chapter 2). One branch of this interest has extended to consider the importance of men's care in parenting. The psychology of moral development has been hampered by its blinkered focus on moral reasoning, but has given rise to extensive debate through Carol Gilligan's (1982) gendered critique of Lawrence Kohlberg's earlier stage-based theory of moral reasoning (1976). Gilligan's argument for a care voice, predominantly heard in girls' and women's moral reasoning, in contrast to the justice voice privileged in Kohlberg's highest stage of moral development, created a central space in feminist theory for the idea of gendered differences in an ethics of care; theory that embraced the disciplines of philosophy, political science, social policy and sociology as well as psychology and psychoanalysis (see Chapter 2).

Feminist philosophers and social theorists have been intent on pursuing a feminist ethics beyond the Kantian sphere of autonomy and justice and into the sphere of interdependence, relationality and care. This interest has extended beyond feminism. Emmanuel Levinas' philosophy (1961/1969, 1974/1981, 1985/1999) takes the ethical relationship as central to subjectivity and responsibility for the Other. Following Michel Foucault's (1988) lead, interest has flourished in care of the self, albeit largely in the generalising way so characteristic of philosophical argument [see Roseneil (2007 unpublished) for an exception]. The political science angle on care ethics, notably Joan Tronto's (1993) and Selma Sevenhuijsen's (1998) work, has the strength of making links to large-scale political issues, such as the boundaries between the public and private spheres and the question of how care ethics work beyond the intimate, or at least interpersonal, sphere, across social distance.

Fiona Williams has identified Joan Tronto and Selma Sevenhuijsen, feminist political scientists, as exemplifying a 'second wave' of work in the ethics of care (Williams 2001), with the first wave being triggered by Gilligan. The second wave is characterised by an attempt to 'resolve the tensions between an ethics of care and an ethic of justice rather than to understand them as a gendered binary' (ibid: 12). In the words of Sasha Roseneil:

> [M]any feminists have expressed reservations about the whole-hearted embracing of an ethics of care, regarding it as over-reliant on a model of care developed from thinking about the fundamentally gendered care practices of mothers for their children, and fearing that it brings with it a diminution of concern about the ethics of justice and social equality. . . . We should be wary that advocating an ethics of care might involve endorsing a model of self which is so fundamentally relational that any sense of individuality, separateness, and capacity to act autonomously is negated.
>
> (Roseneil 2004: 414)

Tronto and Sevenhuijsen are engaging with a tradition of theorising ethics within the polis, a public space that belonged to men and is even now usually defined in opposition to the home (the location of mothering and care). In political science discourse, the idea of distributive justice has dominated. Sevenhuijsen (1998) pursues its implications into the sphere of policy and politics, demonstrating how care can be placed within conceptions of democratic citizenship. She argues that it is possible to transcend the binary of care and justice by going beyond the model of distributive justice with its 'abstract rationality, impartiality and sameness' (1998: 145) and instead focus on practices in the context of power and domination.[4] Once 'care' is not constricted by the motherhood paradigm, it can be seen, she claims, as structuring all human relationships, which includes political and public settings. Both Tronto and Sevenhuijsen emphasise care as a practice. Sevenhuijsen claims that 'the core idea of the ethic of care in my view is that care is a practice, and that it is crucial for developing a moral attitude – and thus also a moral vocabulary – of care by engaging in the practice of care. By doing so care can in fact grow into a disposition, a part of our everyday thinking and doing' (2003: 18). Tronto follows in a long line of theorists, starting with Aristotle for whom 'a good polis was no guarantee that citizens would be ethical, but [. . .] it was almost impossible that good men could exist in a bad polis' (Tronto 1993: 7).

But what understanding of subjectivity underlies these arguments? A Kantian model has dominated in political science discourse: autonomous, cognitive, rational; a model that feminist critics have identified as decidedly masculine. In this perspective, ethical practices are a product of correct reasoning. Because of the influence of feminist critiques, political theory has become more aware of the weaknesses of proceeding according to abstract principles. Andrew Dobson (2006), a political theorist of cosmopolitanism as well as an environmentalist, raises a similar set of questions that result in him advancing a situated and embodied account of obligation and justice: 'thick cosmopolitanism'. He addresses cosmopolitanism's principle that the scope of political obligations is universal and diagnoses its weakness as being because it is based on a 'thin' definition of what connects people together in a common humanity. This leaves, in his view, a 'motivational vacuum' in explaining how people might meet universal political obligations, or, in my terms, a lack of a theory of subjectivity that accounts for people's capacities to care (or not). This is in part due to the abstracted nature of political discourses of justice, as Dobson refers to when he comments that cosmopolitanism tends to construct 'human creatures as primordially thinking creatures' so that 'becoming a cosmopolitan is fundamentally an intellectual affair' (2006: 19). He wants to 'thicken the ties that bind us to "strangers"' (ibid) in a way that this fails to do and invokes an embodied subjectivity which would help causal responsibility to be conceived 'at-a-distance' (2006: 21). I return to this question in Chapter 6 in ways that I think help to transcend the residual dualism between care (embodied, specific, relational) and justice (abstract, rule-based, intellectual).

The absence of an alternative model of subjectivity also, in my view, compromises Tronto's application of care ethics to politics. I illustrate this by looking at her model of care. Tronto did not problematise the capacity to care. Her only reference to how people might be able to care is towards the end of her book when she says 'in order for these qualities [that is, 'to care for those around one or in one's society'] to become a part of moral conduct, people must engage in both private and public practices that teach them, and reinforce their sense of, these moral concerns' (1993: 178). Sevenhuijsen's argument (above) that the practice of care leads to disposition to care takes this a little further into the domain of subjectivity but leaves it unclear if, how and when, such a process takes place. Tronto draws implicitly on a more simplistic model of social learning to account for moral conduct, reinforced with the idea that practice is a sufficient conveyor of moral values. In this, like many social and political theorists, she reduces subjectivity to an empty category filled by social products. The individual residue is therefore naturalised, as individual–society dualism dictates. As most moral philosophers do, she talks about individuals as members of a general category who show moral concern. Often, she implies that if the political barriers to a care ethic were removed (by shifting moral boundaries that currently exist, for example between public and private) then people would naturally care ('from the perspective of care, individuals are presumed to be in a state of moral engagement'; 1993: 164). This naturalisation of care is a blind-spot in the literature about care ethics. If a 'good polis is no guarantee of ethical practices' what *does* create ethical citizens? In Fisher and Tronto's initial work (1990), five 'values of caring' defined caring: attentiveness, responsibility, nurturance, compassion and meeting the other's needs (also in Tronto 1993: 3).[5] I will discuss the three concepts that could potentially provide the conceptual resources for underpinning the capacity to care with a theorisation of subjectivity – meeting needs, attentiveness and compassion – and in the course of a brief critique, signal the ways that I develop these ideas in subsequent chapters.

Meeting needs, attentiveness and compassion

The idea that someone could desire to make themselves dependent on another's preparedness to meet their needs when this was objectively unnecessary is quite foreign to Tronto's way of thinking in *Moral boundaries*. On the one hand, she reflects upon the individualistic culture of the USA and its effects of making autonomy a possible and desirable aspiration. On the other, she believes that the possible and desirable state that care is always aimed towards is that of autonomy, when care is no longer needed. For example, she subscribes to 'the reality that human beings . . . manage to become autonomous' and that 'we can probably assert that one of the goals of care is to end dependence' (1993: 163). Her critique of individualism and autonomy does not actually lead to a different conceptualisation of subjectivity despite her claim to adopt the principle of interdependence. For her, interdependence seems to mean that there will be different times of life when one will be able to extend care or need to receive care. At those times, she implies that the roles are fixed because they are related to physical needs that are ameliorable: at a given time, one is either caring or cared for.

This set of rather covert assumptions in Tronto's treatment of care ethics ignores the existence of fundamental human needs that are relational, like the needs for recognition and trust[6] that exist throughout life, independently of the ebb and flow of our physical capacities to cater for our own needs. Ironically, Tronto remains on the territory of the enlightenment subject of moral rationality that was so influential, through Kant, in traditional moral and ethical theory, a perspective that she explicitly criticises. My analysis of intersubjectivity is very different from her interpersonal model that posits communication between two or more autonomous unitary rational individuals who occasionally need help from others.

A theory of subjectivity premised on the dynamic unconscious intersubjective flow of affect, identification and recognition between people means that care is the psychological equivalent to our need to breathe unpolluted air. We can survive, perhaps for a long time, in polluted air but it damages our vitality, we have to make do and adapt to less. Moreover, good-enough care, like good-enough air, is inside and outside us – inevitably – all the time, whether in its presence or lack. This also means that participating in the daily flow of care, in private and public domains, with intimates and strangers, is not necessarily separate from pleasure and creativity, as Tronto claims (1993: 104). In claiming this, she reproduces the common feminist conflict between caring for others versus self care or looking after one's own needs.[7] Growing out of a primary opposition to women's subordination, feminism has often, understandably, equated women's caring with self-sacrifice. Conflicts between my needs and/or wants and those of someone else I care about exist as a frequent, continuous and inevitable part of life. However, to recognise this is not the same as conceptualising others and self as representing mutually opposed interests. It is simply a part of the experience of conflict between multiple possibilities which is the stuff of existence.

The idea of a primary or necessary opposition of interests between self and others not only derives from an individualistic ontology, it also renders invisible the profound pleasure of the kind of caring that is woven into the fabric of daily life. I don't want to restrict this claim to the performance of activities that can afford enjoyment to a carer (playing with a toddler, taking a convalescent on a day trip, reading a novel out loud to a blind person), nor simply pleasure in one's own altruism. From an intersubjective perspective, a virtuous circle of care can be established whereby a person can take pleasure in another's pleasure who also reciprocates. Someone who is being cared for, even if they are quite dependent, is potentially still capable of many forms of caring, perhaps psychological rather than physical, for example to elicit and pay attention to the state of mind of the carer, to share relevant experience, to express appreciation, thus recognising the other. Sevenhuijsen gives an example of a care worker with elderly people suffering from senile dementia who was quoted in a Dutch newspaper as saying that hearing a word for the first time from one old woman 'makes my morning worthwhile'. Among her characteristics of care – patience, empathy, attentiveness, intimacy – Sevenhuijsen therefore adds 'not least, the ability to draw satisfaction from fulfilling what may seem to be insignificant needs' (1998: 1).

I agree with Sevenhuijsen, that needs are 'the quintessential object of care' (1998: 137) but they are rarely transparent and therefore demonstrate all the complex ways in which caring for depends on qualities of caring about involving attentiveness and compassion. From a psychoanalytic perspective, needs are rarely fixed essential qualities that reasonably need meeting through care. Some needs will turn out to be more or less objective, such as when an old person can no longer reach his or her toenails to cut them, and the care response should be similarly clear cut. The needs of sick people come into this important category. But it is impossible to separate the practices of meeting needs from the psychological meanings, imported from many quarters, which even simple acts will carry. As I show throughout this book, any relationship carries with it the meanings that have built up through the life histories of both parties. These are held in their internal worlds and are transferred to some extent on to any new relationship.

Care relations are, of course, particularly subject to such dynamics, being key to the original foundation of intersubjectivity between infant and mother, or other primary carer. Thus physical needs that are the object of nursing care should not be separated from the whole relationship within which those needs and care are being expressed. For example, in paid care, 'the disclosure of nurses' embodied, emotional involvement . . . enables connection with the patient's experience and well-being, and . . . produces the refinements of physical ministration that alleviate suffering, create the trust that subjectivity will not be betrayed' (Gadow 1990, cited in Bowden 1997: 116).

To complicate matters further, the meeting of needs can be more harmful than helpful. For example, it is not unusual for the expression of needs for care to contain an omnipotent wish to control the other and one's environment; a wish left over from infancy, where it was useful for survival. I discuss the role of omnipotence in thinking and development in Chapters 2 and 3. Such 'needs', if they are met, may grow without limit, so that we hear, for example, of adult men living with their elderly, frail and poor mothers; men who still feel justified in making gross and unlimited demands on their maternal object (and here object is the accurate word). Meeting someone's needs uncritically can result in one's objectification. Omnipotent demands to have one's needs met stem from a failure to develop a capacity to care, which involves seeing the other as a person in her own right.

For Tronto (1993: 121) 'if we are not attentive to the needs of others, then we cannot possibly address these needs'. The absence of attentiveness is therefore a moral failing. She draws from Simone Weil, who 'believed that the capacity for attention was crucial for any genuinely human interaction' (op cit: 127). Sarah Ruddick too regards this to be important, as in her emphasis on 'attentive love' (1989: 118). Selma Sevenhuijsen develops the idea of attention as a crucial feature in care as an ethical practice. She takes Tronto's starting point and develops the idea of caring about, as necessarily preceding caring for but marginalised from political discourse, without which the practices of care lack both 'a heart and a soul' (2002: 10). It is thus important how attentiveness is conceptualised. I agree with Tronto that it is a moral capacity but not one emanating from the will of an intentional rational subject ('the unwillingness of people to direct their attention to others' particular concerns'; 1993: 130). We will not make progress by changing the conditions of possibility for people's attentiveness. These, I argue, reside in the evolving, often unconscious, intersubjective relations that surround someone and are available for identifications and internalisation. Of course, these are expressed in practices and to this extent I share Tronto's and Sevenhuijsen's emphasis on practice, but without Tronto's rationalist and voluntaristic assumptions.

Recent psychoanalysis understands attention and, more broadly, 'thinking about' as developing relationally. An individual's developing capacity for realising and linking thoughts depends on that person internalising a model of containment that makes the emotional content of thinking bearable. If the individual is unable to do so because the accompanying feelings are insufficiently contained to be bearable, then he or she will not be able to be attentive to whatever particular object is involved. Thoughts potentially pose threats to the thinker whether they are about people or not (see my account of Bion's theory of thinking, Chapter 2), but given how closely our subjectivity is tied in with our relationships to others, it is particularly challenging to notice other people's states of mind and how these might implicate one's own conduct. The capacity to do so is not a natural given and so I provide a developmental account of how this is achieved (or fails to be achieved).

Like most social scientists, Tronto excludes a developmental perspective from her analysis. This has become a dominant feature of the social sciences since the 'turn to language', with its accompanying critique of developmental psychology [see in particular the 'new sociology of childhood', for example, Smart *et al.* (2001)]. Although the critique was needed, unfortunately the baby of development has been thrown out with the bathwater of developmentalism. This is compounded by a feminist reluctance to privilege the mother–child relationship as a paradigm of care; for example 'too often, care is described and defined as a necessary relationship between two individuals, most often a mother and child' (Tronto 1993: 103). In contrast, I hope to show in this book how crucial the early primary relationship between mother and infant is for the capacity to care of both of these parties, a relationship that is not so much paradigmatic as originary. I hope also to show how care can, and does, extend from such beginnings to potentially all relationships, even across social distance. Of course, its character changes in the process.

In Tronto's treatment, compassion figures in the context of other theorists' distinctions, which she wishes to transcend, between care and justice ethics where 'care draws out of compassion, justice out of rationality' (1993: 166). It is referred to only in a common-sense way. In my view, compassionate caring about depends on accurate recognition. How this is achieved is addressed in the psycho-analytic concept of identification. Tronto has quite a lot to say about identification, but each time draws on a misleading critique that equates identification with what she refers to as 'overidentification'; that is, a dynamic where a carer loses the capacity to recognise the difference between his or her own needs and those of someone in need of his or her care. In contrast, I use the concept of identification in the psychoanalytic sense to describe the developmental processes that involve the internalisation of identifications with primary carers during the early years and which, when positive, can lay the foundations of the self and for later care from the position of being a person in one's own right (see Chapter 3).

A focus on the capacity to care means that we ask how this relation to another person is achieved. The psychoanalytic concept of identification embraces processes that are conscious and unconscious, embodied, affective and cognitive, both primary (unthought) and secondary (thought) processes. Without the psychological capacity to identify with others across the boundary that comes to define one individual from another, compassion and concern would be impossible. We can only know what another person is experiencing through empathy or 'fellow feeling'; that is, through using ourselves as an instrument of understanding. The capacity for empathy goes far beyond cognitive-based understanding. It involves, for example, imaginatively flinching at the other's response to a cold hand, a sharp needle or an overhot drink and therefore being able to modify one's actions. It involves psychologically imagining oneself in another's position.

The capacity for accurate identification is constantly in danger of being compromised by the unwitting defences we are likely to mobilise in the face of painful feelings. Faced, for example, with a dying person who will not or cannot talk about death, how possible is it not to let one's own fear of dying get in the way of experiencing what they are going through? If that person wishes to finish his or her life quickly, how does a carer separate out their own wishes from those of the other – to keep the loved one for ever, to get rid of him or her to obliterate the obligation to care, or perhaps both at once? How does one recognise and respect the difference between concluding, for example, 'if I were in their shoes, I would want to quit life now before my dignity was completely in shreds' (an example of what Tronto might call 'overidentification') and picking up the signals that, no, they might have thought that earlier but now they want to live every last day? Tronto's inadequate use of the concept of identification reflects a wider and enduring tension in the feminist literature between the idea that identification means feeling the same as (identity with) the other and acknowledging – and respecting – differences. She does this, for example, in her discussion of responsiveness where she claims that putting oneself into another's position presumes that 'the other is exactly like the self' (op cit: 136). These need not be in contradiction if the concept of identification draws on the complexity that contemporary psychoanalysis provides (see Chapter 6).

Psycho-social subjectivity in care

I have concentrated my critique on Tronto because of her importance in taking the care ethics debate away from the mother–child paradigm and into the public sphere, addressing justice. However, the 'second wave' of care ethics has a wider focus too, if it includes, as I think it should, the work of the group gathered within the University of Leeds CAVA project, directed by Fiona Williams. This work, with social policy issues at its core, is also committed to bringing care out of the private sphere, critically analysing the (gendered) power relations involved, factoring in the effects of changing family structures, gender relations and individualisation and engaging with political movements involving marginalised groups such as disability rights and self-help. I situate my work in this book at the psycho-social edge of this second wave.

Williams points out that, from a social policy perspective, care is a powerful analytic concept in times of changing welfare regimes because these point to changes in the relations between state, family, market and voluntary sectors as care providers; to tensions between cash and services modes of provision and who receives this – carer or cared for; and to broad changes in and between demographic and gender relations in care work (2001: 2). She provides an example of how the British disability movement's questioning of relations between carer and cared for challenges basic assumptions about 'the very notion of care' (ibid: 10). This arises out of a history of experience of paid and unpaid carers who have positioned them as dependent, 'at worst abused and stripped of their dignity, at best patronised and protected from exercising any agency over their lives' (2001: 10). Clearly, care has earned a bad name because it has been tainted by unequal power relations, expressed in a model of dependency. Disability activists are thus calling for independence and control over their own lives (ibid). As Froggett noted (above), this contestation points to the importance of considering caring about as well as caring for and addressing the quality of care in psychological, rather than just physical and social terms.

Roseneil, a member of the CAVA group, argues that care in social policy needs re-imagining and uses 'the epistemological challenge offered by queer theory to propose a different gaze be cast on care which recognizes the practices of care which take place outside normative heterosexual couples and families' (2004: 409). She has consequently used a model of friendship as a basis for her research into care relations (ibid). My approach, although informed by a similar critique, does not abandon the mother–child model because, as I hope to show, it reflects fundamental aspects of the way that caring selves develop; aspects that are modified to a greater or lesser extent in adult relationships but which nonetheless form the ground on which caring about is built and infuses practices. It should still be possible to transcend the binary between autonomy, independence and the ethic of justice on the one hand and relationality, empathy and the ethic of care on the other in understanding the capacity to care.

With the exception of psychoanalysis, most of the influential contributions to debates about care lack a psychology, notably a full, critically based theorisation of the self, and its relational development, on which the capacity to care is founded. Developmental psychoanalysis turns out to be the most theoretically fertile area for understanding the relational acquisition of capacities to care and also gets closest in subject matter, for example, through Klein's notion of reparation and Winnicott's understanding of concern. It is also insightful in theorising the effects of sexual and gender difference in the development of care. Psychoanalytic literatures, with the important exception of Winnicott, hardly use the word care. However, they do provide a detailed account of the qualities required by the primary carer in her relationship with the dependent baby if it is to thrive. They also theorise the way these qualities become part of the baby's potential, change with major events in growing up – for example, the processes of establishing a gender identity – and how they mark the quality of relationships with others throughout life.

In my use of psychoanalysis, I draw on the work of Melanie Klein, Fred Alford, Jessica Benjamin, Donald Winnicott, Wilfred Bion, Thomas Ogden, Ron Britton, Juliet Mitchell, the British school of object relations and the American relational psychoanalysts. Attachment theory, which originated with John Bowlby's work, has also been highly influential in establishing as commonplace the significance to later psychological well-being of attachment relationship between babies and primary carer. In its later empirical manifestations (Ainsworth *et al.* 1974, 1978, Main 1993) it has established these central claims and also refined its theoretical principles in the direction of an emphasis on intersubjectivity (Diamond and Marrone 2003).These literatures draw attention to the importance of relationships in understanding care, not just in the obvious sense – care is a relational term – but in the sense that the individual, caring (and careless) subject is constituted relationally, right through to the deepest most hidden parts of their subjectivity. The processes and the product are ethical in their very nature. I use the term 'unconscious intersubjectivity' to refer to this idea. The foreword to Diamond and Marrone's book *Attachment and intersubjectivity* begins by commenting that 'The term "intersubjectivity" has become contemporary shorthand for a variety of attempts to transcend an intrapsychic model of the mind' (2003: vii). Such attempts have become so common in the last fifty years that they amount to a transdisciplinary paradigm shift. The term has developed in three different disciplinary areas: phenomenology, psychoanalysis and developmental psychology. I draw in particular on the last two. Many of the emphases of phenomenology are compatible with my emphasis, namely the view that 'existence is interpersonal from the first and always profoundly related to context' (Diamond and Marrone 2003: 13). A psychoanalytic perspective treats intersubjectivity as an unconscious flowing of states between people and modifying them. It thus raises questions about the psychological boundaries between people.

Events in the external world are not just mediated by language or discourse but, importantly, by people's states of mind. By this I do not refer to cognitive processes but to 'mental states' or 'internal worlds' where desire and anxiety act creatively on experience and transform it, so that its relation to reality can never be simply assumed. The idea of an internal world refers, in object relations theory, to a world of unconscious fantasy made up of the self and other internal objects such as people, things, ideas and values (Fakhry Davids 2002: 67). This world 'provides a template for our interactions with the outside world, is itself shaped by these, and is the wellspring of our psychic well-being and of creativity itself' (ibid). I use the term 'intersubjectivity' in this sense.

Emmanuel Levinas' project to found philosophy on an ethics based on an interhuman order is part of the phenomenological tradition: 'a phenomenology of sociality' (Levinas 1999: 103). This has been influential in placing ethics at the heart of philosophy. Hayat, introducing Levinas' *Alterity and transcendence* (1999), puts the point as follows: 'a philosophy of dialogue cannot not be an ethics . . . like Buber for whom the beginning of philosophy is not the cogito but the relation to the other' (Levinas 1999: xxi). Likewise, an analysis of the capacity to care cannot not be a contribution to theorising ethical subjectivity.

My approach also emphasises the importance of life history to the capacity to care. In other words, it is developmental. In thinking developmentally I aim to focus on the 'dynamics of becoming' (Loewald 1980: 6). Development is not seen here in the way that developmentalism has been criticised, that is, for viewing it as fixed, staged and normative (Burman 1994), but in the sense that people are a product of their pasts and that we cannot choose to leave behind how these have forged us, although changes continue. Ben Bradley (1989) shows that developmental visions of infancy tend to fall into two kinds: foundational or constructionist. Foundational accounts are based on the belief that babies have real limitations that change over time with experience. Constructionist accounts of infancy show the ways that different theories have been imposed on what is posited as a 'blank slate'. This is a dualism that I attempt to transcend in what I would call a critical realist approach to infant and child development: attempting to show how theories have constructed infancy and also to assess which ones best answer my underlying question 'can this theory give me any insight into the capacity to care?'.

The same critical realist approach characterises my treatment of mothering and here any version of realism is likely to run into political controversy linked to the value judgements that come with it; for example about the compromised care that depressed mothers are likely to be able to provide for their babies. Certainly, part of my project in this book is to go beyond the kind of relativism that recognises no real effects of development or mothering but treats solely discursive effects. At their most inadequate, these are the kinds of discourses that allow one to argue that oppressive discourses have kept mothers constrained entirely for patriarchal purposes and that the quality of maternal care has no actual effects on babies' well-being. My critical realism attempts to recognise the effects of such ideologies on women's subjectification and, at the same time, make some realist arguments about what kinds of care babies are likely to need. An example would be the way I make a distinction between the biological mother and 'maternal care' provided by others, and also explore carefully what connections there may be between babies' experiences of the biological mother and other maternal figures and why.

My care ideal is that adults can engage in four kinds of care. First, they will be capable of reciprocal, interdependent care receiving and care giving. Second, they will be capable of providing the non-negotiable, asymmetrical demand for care that has always been required of mothers and is required of fathers and others who 'mother' babies and young children. Third, they will be capable of self care. Fourth, they will be capable of extending their care to both human and non-human objects (for example, the environment or non-human animals), including outside their direct experience. Understanding how these are achieved entails understanding the vicissitudes of the development of mind, self and morality. It will become clear that there are many variations on capacity to care and many conditions that risk the failure of good-enough capacity to care.

Outline of the book

Chapter 1: Introducing the capacity to care   The current chapter has set the scene for my particular approach by discussing its contemporary relevance and situating the capacity to care briefly in existing literature. I identify a significant gap in addressing capacities to care and their acquisition psychologically. I make some initial links to the policy questions in which care is a central consideration. Tronto's widely cited account of the constituents of care was useful to introduce why and how a psycho-social perspective on subjectivity takes issue with dominant assumptions about how people care, to signal my different theoretical emphases and to introduce the core themes of my account. I have referred to ideas about people's capacity to care that are based on a radically different ontology from that which is dominant in Western culture and Western social science, the latter being based on assumptions of a bounded autonomous individual. Feminist theory has been at the forefront of a critique of this ontology, notably through conceptualisations of care and care ethics.

Chapter 2: Care, ethics and relational subjectivity　The literatures that could most be expected to address and understand the capacity to care in a moral and gendered framework are the feminist literatures, first on the ethic of care and second on the reproduction of caring through the mother–daughter relationship. In this chapter I review these, aiming to specify their strengths, weaknesses and blind spots. I draw on the developmental psychoanalytic emphasis on unconscious intersubjectivity through the concepts of identification, conflict, differentiation and recognition, to provide a modified account of gender differences in moral reasoning and the ethics of care and justice. My account foregrounds Fred Alford's concept of reparative reasoning (based on Melanie Klein's notion of reparation) and uses Wilfred Bion's work to go beyond the cognitive traditions of theorising thinking and attention. I demonstrate the need to transcend a gendered binary between separation/autonomy and connectedness/ relatedness, in recognition of the fluid, non-essential, character of gender subjectivity, particularly in the contemporary context of greater gender flexibility.

Chapter 3: Intersubjectivity in self development　Babies' potential to develop caring capacities lies in the intersubjectivity of their mental states and their absolute need for care from a familiar and dependable person. If and how they develop the capacity to care is fundamentally dependent on intersubjective processes, and this chapter describes and theorises these in terms of babies' developing selves, unconscious intersubjective dynamics and how meaning is made of their experience, especially prior to language development. Central is how they develop the ability to imagine and identify with another's state of mind. I trace the developmental struggles through which moral subjectivity is achieved. My understanding of moral subjectivity is based on Kleinian and post-Kleinian, especially Winnicottian, concepts. I ground much of this in a brief and simple example of a two-year-old boy, Carl, who makes a caring gesture to his harassed mother when her self control breaks down.

In this chapter I set up a related cluster of themes for elaboration in subsequent chapters. I ask how a child differentiates, or separates, from its mother or primary carer and how sex and gender affect these processes. I suggest that the carer's recognition of the baby's states of mind is important in how the baby learns recognition, with effects on subjectivity and capacity to care. I introduce Bion's concepts of the container and contained as a non-cognitive model for learning how to think and its implications for attentiveness. An illustration from a longitudinal baby observation provides the basis for inferring the internalisation of a parental good object and I consider how this is the basis for feelings of self worth and by extension the capacity for self care. In this argument, self care and care for others stem from the same source, rather than being in conflict. I discuss a question that is central to a psycho-social approach to subjectivity: the relation between the external reality that the baby meets and the inner psychic processes (for example splitting) that transform that reality and produce experience and meaning. Last but not least, I broaden out the focus on the mother–infant couple to introduce the role of dyadic and triangular structures in babies' development of 'mental space' and the role of siblings in the development of ethical subjectivity.

Chapter 4: Maternal subjectivity and the capacity to care In this chapter I hold in balance the universal demands of being a mother, namely the non-negotiable character of the new infant's dependency, and the situation of the woman who is never only a mother. I try to unsettle the binary of other- versus self-centredness in discourses that have characterised women's positions as mothers. I characterise the move into maternal subjectivity as a way of confronting, and potentially living up to, the challenges of caring for others in a dynamic way from the position of being a subject in her own right. Maternal subjectivity is forged out of the love, demands and responsibilities that help a baby move out of undifferentiation, omnipotence and narcissism – from a state of 'ruthlessness' (Winnicott) – to the capacity to feel realistic concern for, and therefore be able to care for, another person. The demands change continuously with the child's development, from one-way care to – ideally – a situation of mutual recognition and interdependency that characterises many other care scenarios. These dynamics of maternal development are not restricted to biological mothers.

Early mothering is a time that reemphasises, par excellence, the dynamic tension between intersubjectivity – on which condition in the mother the new baby relies for its psychological well-being – and differentiated subjectivity or individuality. I use Ogden's concept of the intersubjective third to explore this tension and how it can provide a way of understanding selves. I argue that the capacities born out of this dialectic can expand beyond being an actual mother or woman and provide the basis for ethical life. This is different from the valorisation of the feminine that characterised some 1980s feminisms in that it does not reserve these characteristics for women but explores how these capacities can be generalised through caring relationships, especially in the context of the unsettling of gender differences.

Chapter 5: The gender of parenting, the gender of care In this chapter I ask what might be specific to the position of a biological mother and if and how might this differ from the father's position in relation to the demands of young children. At the same time I address one political question that provides a backdrop to this book;

20

namely 'what difference might it make if fathers rather than mothers were the primary carers for babies and children?' To this extent, this chapter focuses on men and boys and what, in their current development, may restrict their capacity to care. I take an intergenerational approach by keeping in mind the parenting conditions that are likely to affect the development of boys' gendered subjectivity and thus their later parental capacities to care. I ask what is particular about the (biological) mother's body, women's and men's bodies and their differences and how the infant and later child might experience these differences. For this purpose I draw on psychoanalytic work that theorises the importance of the earliest relations experienced in the mode of embodiment rather than thought or language, for later subjectivity, relationality and identificatory capacity. I conclude that the mother's and father's bodies cannot signify the same in the infant's early experience. Likewise the 'fantasy of the omnipotent mother' will not generalise to men's mothering without profound changes in its meaning and the child's experience.

Shifting focus from the sex and gender of the parents to that of the children, I draw on Jessica Benjamin's understanding of pre-Oedipal as well as Oedipal dynamics, and in particular her distinction between the intersubjective conditions that help a boy to renounce, as opposed to repudiate, his mother in the course of separation. From this, using the idea of cross-sex and cross-gender parental identifications, it is possible to understand how the defensively autonomous character structures typical of masculinity can be modified, affecting men's capacities to care. Finally, I move beyond dyadic relationships using the emphasis in contemporary psycho-analysis on triangularity, the third term and the analytic third in order to complicate the question of what children need so as to develop the capacity to imagine themselves in the position of the other. I introduce sibling relationships into the family picture, showing their influence in the experiencing of love and hate, particularly on lateral relationships.

Chapter 6: Difference and the capacity to care   Throughout the book, the concept of identification has been central to theorising the capacity to care and here I try to untangle a common conflation between identification and sameness by discussing the conditions for identification with differences as well as similarities. I apply the psycho-social intersubjective model of the caring self that I have developed in this book to several scenarios that diverge from the face-to-face and familiar basis to unconscious intersubjectivity derived from the mother-infant couple. These cover friendship, institutional care and caring across social difference and across distance.

The chapter widens the focus to discuss the subject of ethics in the light of my theorisation of the capacity to care and its origins in the mother–infant relationship. This takes two directions. In the light of the radically intersubjective ontology I have developed throughout the book, I further consider Levinas' similar ontology; also the friendship model of care as an alternative and complement to the mother–child model. To test how my approach extends from the intimacy of primary face-to-face relations, I ask if and how the capacity to care extends to apply to other settings, namely institutional care and charitable giving to third world countries. In this way I return to the question of justice and the role of motivations to care in political obligations. Once defensive autonomy and instrumental reasoning are distinguished clearly from justice reasoning, the care–justice dualism is further unsettled.

2

CARE, ETHICS AND RELATIONAL SUBJECTIVITY

The experience of the mother as a separate being [is] perhaps the single most important [developmental] step we will ever take.

(Alford 2002: 41)

How can she [the daughter] separate psychically from the mother without entering into another relationship where she relinquishes her will and desire?

(Maguire 1995: 61)

The model of self behind the ethic of care

A major influential strand of feminist writing in the last twenty-five years has been the attempt to redefine theories of the self (also referred to as 'subjectivity', 'the subject' and 'identity') to reflect a feminine, caring, rather than a masculine, norm. In philosophy, this has entailed a critique of the Kantian, Enlightenment principle of the autonomous, independent, self-interested, individualistic subject in favour of a connected, relational, caring subject who is formed and embedded in social relationships and whose ethics are defined by care for others (Mackenzie and Stoljar 2000). In critical psychology, a parallel critique focused on how twentieth-century psychology espoused a similar model of the individual (Henriques *et al.* 1984). Feminist theory has been most active on this terrain, based on its commitment to critiquing the way that the universal human subject is in fact a masculine one.

Three texts, all North American, are outstanding exemplars of this strand of feminism. First, Nancy Chodorow's (1978) *The reproduction of mothering*, set the terms for the subsequent debate about shared parenting by providing an explanation for how girls grow up to be more engaged in care than boys (because mothers, not fathers, are primarily engaged in their care). Second, Carol Gilligan's (1982) *In a different voice* conducted a feminist critique of a psychology of the development of moral reasoning, which led to the unsettling of a whole masculinist philosophy of ethics based on abstract principles of justice. Gilligan argued that an ethic of care was as important as an ethic of justice and thus introduced what has become a veritable industry in feminist academia concerning care and care ethics.[1] The third classic was the result of going beyond the first decade of this work. Joan Tronto's *Moral boundaries* (1993) (see Chapter 1) is a book that took the principle of an ethic of care into the terrain of political science and argued that care should not be confined to women or the private sphere but be central to all of human life. During this time, feminist theory and research, from psychoanalysis and critical psychology to sociology and social policy, from moral philosophy and politics to social work and nursing, has engaged with the related notions of care ethics, gender difference and how to theorise subjectivity to embrace the kinds of morality that are usually taken to be more typical of women than men.

These writings have not directly addressed the capacity to care and few have lingered on the detailed questions of how to theorise subjectivity once the notion of the autonomous individual subject is called into question. The principle of relational subjectivity has become widely accepted, the idea of interdependence is preferred over independence, but few writers have engaged with the detailed questions I am asking in this book: how does a narcissistic infant acquire and fail to acquire the capacity to care for others? How do they and the adults they become differentiate between their own wishes and those of others? How does inter-subjectivity actually work? How do these processes differ for girls and boys, for mothers and fathers?

Because much of the care literature is written in a philosophical mode, claims are made about care that are not examined in relation to psychological knowledge about selves in relation to others. It will take the whole of this book to set out a fuller theorisation of relational subjectivity or intersubjectivity and its implications for the capacity to care.[2] In this chapter I discuss the parts of the ethics of care literature with a psychological focus, in particular Gilligan's foundational work, aiming to take the debate forward by unpicking the binary thinking that sees relationality and connectedness as opposed to autonomy and separateness and considering how these capacities extend to the ethics of care and justice.

In particular, this part of the feminist ethic of care literature has concerned itself with the gendered nature of care, notably the way that maternal care is reproduced in the mother–daughter relationship and the way that girls' and boys' thinking about care is gender differentiated. My main interest in returning to this literature is to examine the model of the self, its gendered, moral development and the assumptions about thinking that underpin these. The idea of a gendered split between boys and girls, where boys achieve separation and autonomy and girls remain in connected-ness, initially with their mothers, unites both early Chodorow and Gilligan and has been an influential theme in feminist theories of gender development. I show how it is possible to go beyond this binary and argue for the importance, in contemporary late modern cultures, of separation and differentiation in the development of all children, usually in relation initially to their mothers. For these purposes, I draw on the British object relations tradition in psychoanalysis that starts with Melanie Klein and includes Donald Winnicott and Wilfred Bion.

It is telling that the development of aspects of girls' Oedipal and separation conflicts appears to occur later, or in a more protracted fashion, than boys'; namely in adolescence, which coincides with Gilligan's – and others' – findings about girls' 'loss of voice'. In her case study of Amy's and Jake's moral reasoning, Gilligan found gendered differences between an ethic of care and an ethic of justice. I introduce Fred Alford's contrast between instrumental and reparative reasoning and bring this into play with Bion's theory of the emotional basis of thought in order to help to account for the gendered nature of differences in thinking. Central to Bion's ideas is the postulate that all infants must give up omnipotence in their thinking and come to terms with the realities that they encounter in acting upon the outside world. Omnipotence can compromise instrumental thinking and ethics of justice. Alford puts forward reparative reasoning as the basis of 'caritas', that is, care. As long as gender differences are distinguished from sex differences, as I do in my argument, it is possible to explain gender differences in ethics of care. The explanation relies on a radically intersubjective concept of self and self development that has been lacking even from feminist accounts that emphasise relationships.

Women's care as mothers

Women's care as mothers has been an enduring topic of concern for feminist thought, usually approached as a problem, as a site of women's oppression. The legacy goes back as far as Simone de Beauvoir's (1949/1972) *The second sex*. She, of all feminists, was perhaps the most vitriolic about motherhood, arguing that the mother's feeling of being a valuable human being 'is only an illusion' (1949/1972: 513), that pregnancy is 'gratuitous cellular growth' and 'a brute fact of nature' (1949/1972: 514). Susan Hekman (1999: 7) characterises de Beauvoir's strategy for feminism, like that of Shulamith Firestone (1970), as the 'erasure of difference and the pursuit of equality'. In other words, women had to become like men. Their analysis of the obstacles was based on women's biology. Nancy Chodorow and Carol Gilligan represent a second strategy, that of valorising the feminine. By this time, the late 1970s and early 1980s, respectively, feminist analysis had shifted decisively to emphasising the social, in practice the relational, sources of women's subordination.

In 1978, Chodorow identified women's care as mothers as the central feature of the reproduction of gender difference and thereby of gender inequality. Because women's and men's care for children is asymmetrical, girls grow up identifying with their mothers as carers and reproduce women-as-carers. In political terms, Chodorow's conclusion was that childcare not equally shared between women and men was a problem that needed changing.[3] Girls grow up to be good at relationships, whereas boys, pushed away earlier than girls by the mother and identifying with a cultural ideal of masculinity in the absence of a day-to-day relationship with their real fathers, grow up good at (defensive) autonomy. Shared parenting would eliminate this basic gender difference, enabling both girls and boys to partake of the advantages of both connectedness and autonomy. This argument, for all that it has been critiqued, refined and transcended, provides one of the pillars for the current emphasis on shared parenting. It suggests that if you change the practices of the real, external parents, gendered subjectivity will follow. Chodorow's subsequent critique of her own position (1989: 7) is that this approach is too sociological and does not allow for the independent effectivity of intrapsychic life on gendered subjectivity. She now prefers a relational theorisation of the individual (1989; Chapter 7).

Girls' relatedness or connectedness was also the central theme of Gilligan's *In a different voice* (1982), in which she argued that it affected the way that girls solved ethical dilemmas. Gilligan's empirical research on girls' and boys' moral reasoning challenged Lawrence Kohlberg's (1976). Based on using ethical dilemma puzzles to assess children's moral reasoning, Kohlberg had devised a stage theory that culminated in the achievement of an abstract, logical form of reasoning based on an ethic of justice. (This is the kind of reasoning that Dobson was problematising in cosmopolitanism's principle of justice based on fair and reasonable treatment to all on the basis of shared membership of common humanity; see Chapter 1.) In this, Kohlberg reflected the modernist moral philosophy of the time, based on the idea of a universal, reliable truth, reached through the capacity to reason. With hindsight, it is not surprising that he found that mainly men reached this pinnacle of moral reasoning: women's and girls' reasoning was often too concrete and qualified to count. Gilligan raised a storm when she challenged the sexism inherent in this hierarchy of morality because she elevated an alternative ethic, the ethic of care, to a status as equal – if not superior[4] – to the ethic of justice.

One of Gilligan's commonly cited examples from *In a different voice*, of the moral reasoning of two eleven-year olds, Jake and Amy, serves to illustrate what are potentially gendered differences in modes of reasoning, which add up to a tendency for boys and men to draw on an ethic of justice and girls and women an ethics of care. The ethical dilemma given to the children is called the 'Heinz dilemma': Heinz's wife will die unless she receives an expensive drug that Heinz cannot afford. The pharmacist will not sell it at a lower price. Should Heinz steal the drug? According to Gilligan, Jake applies a mathematical logic whereby he derives the abstract out of the particular and reasons that there are two moral principles at stake: the value of life and the value of property. He concluded that the value of life should take precedence, which is the 'right' answer according to Kohlberg's scheme. In contrast, Amy's approach involves needing to know more about the particulars before she can come up with the solution that is appropriate to the specific instance: does Heinz love his wife? Has he tried changing the pharmacist's mind? Could he borrow money? Would he go to jail if caught and if so who would look after his wife? Gilligan calls this 'not a math problem with humans but a narrative of relationships that extends over time' (1982: 28).

Gilligan was one of the earliest psychologists to use qualitative methods in her research and thus she was having to invent methodological principles as she went along, for example concerning how one generalises from small numbers of cases and how one draws reliable comparisons between groups (boys and girls in this case). The methodological problems in Gilligan's arguments have been endlessly raked over by psychologists [for example, see Larabee (1993)] and Gilligan's arguments about gender difference in the ethics of care are not clear. However, single-case examples can legitimately be used to do comparative work if extrapolation from the cases proceeds theoretically, as I do in this chapter by analysing the gender difference that is suggested by Jake and Amy's reasoning (and evidenced in many other findings as well), at the same time as accounting for instances when boys manifest care reasoning [see Broughton (1993)].

The 'different voice' of girls and women was the main theme of Gilligan's subsequent work as leader of the Harvard Project (Brown and Gilligan 1993). This work focused entirely on adolescent heterosexual girls and found that, at a point in adolescence that often coincided with the time when they started to have relationships with boys, girls lost the authentic 'voice'[5] that had characterised their earlier thinking and acting in relationships. For example, Gilligan approvingly quotes an adolescent girl, Stephanie, asserting that 'You should tell everybody how you feel, if it won't hurt their feelings, of course' (Gilligan 1991: 17). (Gilligan passes over the contradictory problem that is posed: what do you do when speaking out will hurt someone's feelings?) Actually, the problem that Gilligan calls loss of voice is a commonplace of feminist and psychoanalytic literatures, namely the passivity of women in heterosexual relationships (Gilligan did not explicitly problematise the girls' heterosexuality).[6] From her experience as a psychoanalytic therapist, Maguire (as in the epigraph) poses a similar question but, crucially, without the binary of separation–connection: 'how can she [the daughter] separate psychically from the mother without entering into another relationship where she relinquishes her will and desire?' (1995: 61). Other psychoanalysts identify a similar problem with spontaneity, which is not confined to girls, a 'quality of unrelatedness which represents failure in development of a spontaneous, stable, taken-for-granted self experience' (Bromberg, cited in Frosh 1991: 73).

Likewise, the Harvard Project group claims that 'relationship' (or 'connection') is a crucial component of what is lost, setting up a paradox that Gilligan refers to as 'the taking of oneself out of relationship for the sake of relationships' (Gilligan 1991: 26–27). The 'struggle for connection' (Gilligan 1993: xv) appears as a struggle to retain authentic feelings in the face of pressures from the outside towards inauthenticity and resultant psychological damage. Brown and Gilligan's definition of psychological health resembles spontaneity: 'responding to oneself, knowing one's feelings and thoughts, clarity, courage, openness and free-flowing connections with oneself, with others and the world . . .' (1993: 13). The assumption – one subjected to numerous critiques[7] – is of an authentic inner self, faced with external pressures, rather like in a 1960s human relations model, where feelings are true and socialising influences are compromising and need to be sloughed off. Questions concerning authenticity or true self have become difficult to pose in the face of various critiques, leaving a further lacuna in the understanding of psychological health in girls' (and boys') development and its relationship to their capacity to care. According to Gilligan, the fact that girls' subjectivity is based on relatedness produces the gendered nature of the ethic of care. However, the concepts of relational subjectivity, voice and connectedness as used by Gilligan need further theoretical clarification. I pursue this in what follows, dissatisfied with accounts of subjectivity that give up on integration and authenticity entirely, through the idea of being a subject in one's own right.

According to Hekman (1999), Gilligan's approach to gender difference belongs to the second of the feminist strategies, namely valorising women's difference from men. The work of 'self-in-relation' theorists,[8] represents a cruder expression of this trend, which serves to illustrate its dangers. The central thesis was that female subjectivity develops through relationship and not through separation, whereas the reverse is true of men. The importance of separation to gender development begins in Freud's assertion that, because girls' passage through the Oedipus complex does not involve the need to cut themselves off so decisively from profound dependencies on and desire for the mother, girls do not achieve the same kind of independent, separate, autonomous identity as boys, nor the same kind of moral integrity.[9]

This reversal strategy (valorising what women, rather than what men supposedly are) involved a dismissive critique of the Oedipus complex (and the whole of Freudian drive theory) as 'based on a Hobbesian notion of competition, power, aggression and possession of others as objects' (Jordan 1997: 56; see also Gilligan 2002: 228–231). Consequently, separation was not seen as necessary for development, as in Mahler's (1968) elaboration of Freudian ideas; rather it was dismissed as deriving from a patriarchal model. In contrast, women's relationality was elevated, the core of which was the development of empathy (Jordan *et al.* 1991) within the mother–daughter relationship. Surrey (1991), for example, identifies three components of this: the girl child's wish to maintain connectedness; the consequent development of mutual empathy with the mother and, over time, mutual attunement and sensitivity to feelings. While these features are recognisable in good mother–daughter relationships, they are only part of the picture. Although self-in-relation theory had the merits of recognising that the mother's relationship to son and daughter could be very different, that the mother–child relationship was reciprocal and not one-way and it could therefore glimpse the mother as subject rather than object, it depleted women of a subjectivity that was not dependent on relationships. To throw out Freudian drive theory throws out women's anger and women's independent sexual desire, and to throw out separateness gives up on the possibility that women could survive on their own. Bot and Corbasson comment that 'in trying to present only the positive aspects of womanhood . . . self-in-relation theory loses the full body of the female experience and confines women's expression of themselves to models of goodness, models of empathy' (1998: 425). They also note that it 'treats the concept of separation as if it were dangerous to the survival of womanhood' (1998: 429).

Separation

It is therefore an important aspect of this book to theorise separation in a way that takes it seriously; that does not reduce it to Freud and Lacan's belief that the father's 'law' is essential to interpose between the mother and child to ensure separation, nor entirely reject the role of father (or the mother) in separation. The feminist rejection of Freud's Oedipal theory led to a failure to consider the importance of the father (or other adult 'third term') in children's separation from the mother. As a consequence, American feminist object relations theory has been dominated by a two-person model based on the parent–child (more specifically the mother–daughter) paradigm.

Alongside these relational feminists there were those who continued to consider that the father was important for the girl's separation as well as the boy's. Dorothy Dinnerstein's account in *The rocking of the cradle and the ruling of the world* (1976) emphasised, following Freud, that the particular difficulties for girls in separating from the all-powerful early mother led them to turn to their fathers. Janine Chasseguet-Smirgel, a French psychoanalyst, asserted that, by turning to the father: 'women do not wish to become men but to detach themselves psychically from the mother and become complete autonomous women' (1964/1985: 118, quoted in Maguire 1995: 59). More recently, Jessica Benjamin (1990, 1995) makes careful developmental and analytical distinctions between separation processes and Oedipal processes. She argues that girls can turn to their fathers through a wish to identify with what the father represents, not as a consequence of Oedipal dynamics (which for Freud involved girls' disappointed turning away from the mother because she too lacked a penis and a turning to the father for what she lacked).

In my view, there are two main weaknesses in the Harvard Project and self-in-relation models (which are closer to psychology than psychoanalysis). First, they lack an analysis of unconscious dynamics.[10] With the use of a psychoanalytic perspective, we cannot fail to include unconscious conflictual dynamics. Importantly, these include what Benjamin calls the 'negative moment', not just the empathy, love, understanding or mutuality, but the aggression, the misunderstanding and the competition. This means (Benjamin 1995: 23 footnote 6) that the two ideals of autonomy and connection 'cannot be simply set up as happy complements'. Keeping in mind the negative moment is essential for understanding mother–daughter relations. It is also an important principle in ensuring that an understanding of the capacity to care is not a romanticised one. Second, the Harvard Project saw relationality and connection as the direct opposite of separation. As a result of this binary thinking, Gilligan effects a reversal, so that it is separation that is pathological, or at least unhealthy, and connection (initially to the mother, but serving as a model for all later relationships, particularly among women) is psychologically healthy. The problem in most of the relational feminist literature is that in the absence of theorising connection in a more complex way, it comes to imply that no separation is needed from the mother; that lack of separation is healthy. For example, in adopting the premise 'that we live not in separation but in relationship' (Gilligan 1993: xxvii), Gilligan is using a caricatured idea of separation that appears to deny the need for a baby to differentiate from her mother, thus imposing an unnecessary opposition that distorts her arguments.

Clinical evidence, by contrast, requires that connection be theorised in a way that is not diametrically opposed to separation. As Sheila Ernst puts it:

> The infant's developing identity can most usefully be understood as
> part of a relationship in which, on the one hand there is a need for
> relating, mutuality and recognition and, on the other, a need to negotiate
> a series of separations.
>
> (Ernst 1997: 84)

This non-binary, both/and position regarding the relationship between separation and connectedness transcends the binary logic of the self-in-relation approach while still going beyond Freud's denigration of girls' inevitable lack of autonomy as a result of not having to separate from mother in the way that boys were obliged to do. Ernst's view evolved from the experience of working therapeutically with women[11] and discovering how problematic the mother–daughter relationship could be when failures to separate lead to problems in establishing a differentiated identity (Ernst 1997).

The difference in emphasis between the formulations of the self-in-relation theorists and Ernst is partly a matter of clinical experience but it also exposes a difference between the direction of psychoanalytic theorising in American and British feminism. As I have shown, American feminism – which so influentially set the terms of this debate – drew upon and developed a different version of psychoanalytic object relations theory to the object relations theory that originated in the work of Melanie Klein and developed in Britain. The American version was less unruly and less conflictual, more orientated to happy solutions and focused on the mother–child relationship. In its appropriation by feminism, it lost unconscious conflict, the 'negative moment', and an appreciation of the vicissitudes of the developing self. For example, Gilligan claims that her premise, cited above, that 'we live not in separation, but in relationship' is the premise of object relations theory.

Hekman, a political philosopher, attributes to object relations theory the arguments that defined women as 'peaceful, caring, relational, and nurturing, as opposed to men who are aggressive and autonomous' (1999: 33). There were exceptions, however: as early as 1985, Evelyn Fox Keller, from a critical feminist perspective on the history of science, argued for a distinction between dynamic and static autonomy. The former is connected with the free expression of one's own volition, creativity and an enhanced ability to relate to the world that is 'both differentiated from and related to others' (Fox Keller 1985: 99). Static autonomy, by contrast, is related to the aim of domination and the claims of separateness that it entails are brittle and defensive. Dynamic autonomy is very similar to my subsequent discussion of being a subject in one's own right.

Understanding this debate and its history is important for feminism because it addresses fundamental questions of how women's subjectivity is acquired, how it may be different from men's and the possible fault lines and strengths resulting from the special features of the daughter's relationship to her mother. If relationality or connectedness is assumed to lead to women's capacity to care, it is important to develop a model of separation that is consistent with connectedness. The trouble lies largely with loose use of concepts on both sides of the binary: separation, autonomy versus relationality, connectedness.

In fact, the original object relations thinking of Klein and Winnicott did theorise relation and separation as part of the same process of self development. The starting point of this tradition, unlike Freud, for whom pleasure seeking was the primary principle in human development, was that human infants are primarily object seeking; that is, they need and seek relations with others. Moreover, it is only through others that they can develop a sense of self (something that is, by definition, unique to them). According to Benjamin, infants need recognition, or 'to be known as oneself'. The paradox is that 'at the very moment of realizing our own independence, we are dependent upon another to recognize it' (Benjamin 1984: 293) and so the coexistence of differentiated selfhood and connectedness to others is unlikely to be constantly comfortable because it involves this tension. In the Kleinian and post-Kleinian depth model, the sense of a self as different from the mother is achieved in the same process as the recognition of that other as not just an extension of the self's omnipotent wishes, but as a combination of what is experienced by the infant as good and bad, fulfilling and frustrating. This self becomes separate in the sense that it is based on the capacity to recognise differences, to know what belongs where. It is not separate in the sense of being independent from others for psychological processes such as recognition. It is autonomous in the sense of being capable of acting in interests that are not an unwitting extension of another person's but an expression of one's own wishes (not in the sense of being a unitary, impervious individual). In this light relationality can include the possibility of relating between people who recognise each other as subjects in their own right.

Separation is something that is a developmental challenge for all, starting in babyhood before gender differentiation becomes salient. I concur with Klein (here summarised by Alford) who believed that, although there will be gender differences in the way that the challenge of separation is met, 'these differences pale in comparison to the common task faced by every human being: to integrate love and hate' (Alford 1989: 165). This is not to ignore the role of gender differentiation (see Chapter 5), but it is to try to maintain an analytic balance between gendered and non-gendered processes. I also bear in mind Benjamin's arguments that pre-Oedipal processes are not gender neutral. Just because the baby is not yet facing the threats of loss involved in gender differentiation, it does not mean that parents are not already affecting their babies' experiences in gendered ways, through identification. For example, this would occur if, when the girl turns to her father out of identificatory love, he fails to identify with her because of his own gendered constraints and therefore fails to recognise and respond to her appeal.

In the light of this approach to separation, I want to rescue the term 'autonomy' from its masculinist connotations deriving from the second strategy of feminist thinking described above. Autonomy does not need to be synonymous with the idea of total independence or impermeable boundaries (MacKenzie and Stoljar 2000). It can mean the freedoms (psychic as well as social) to be responsible for my own desires, pleasures and aspirations (some – or perhaps all – of which will, of course, implicate me in my relatedness to others). This requires differentiation because I cannot know clearly my own desires if I have not succeeded in differentiating these from my mother's (and later others'). Once differentiated, my identifications with her and others part of myself. Differentiation and separation are not synonymous (see Chapter 3).

Differentiation is a struggle. Benjamin stresses that there is no resolution to the tensions involved in the desire for recognition: 'the early struggle for recognition . . . includes failure, destruction, aggression, even when it is working' (1995: 23). The need for recognition in itself guarantees relationality as a force in the making of selves. If it is accepted as correct, it is enough to maintain that complete autonomy is an illusion, a defence against the vulnerability of needing, which means being dependent upon others at various moments for recognition. This does not, however, mean that people cannot act independently. It means that human beings have many different needs and desires that are frequently in conflict with each other.

The quality of babies' relationality changes as the baby learns to differentiate from the mother's psyche-soma (Winnicott 1958). If things go well enough, that child will eventually be able to engage in what Benjamin calls 'subject–subject relations', which involve two people who are subjects in their own right. From this position – in popular speech, we might call it 'being my own person' – I can be connected to another person. Without it connection would not be connection at all but lack of differentiation. Undifferentiation is understood in psychoanalysis to be a continuation of infants' phantasied omnipotence, untempered by coming to terms with the separate reality of other subjects: 'In this state we are unable to take in that the other person does not want what we want, do what we say' (Benjamin 1998: 86). It is a state associated with violence and antithetical to good enough care because it would be based on a failure to distinguish one's own needs from the other's needs in the caring relationship.

Boys' and girls' Oedipal conflict

In Chapter 5, I argue that the Oedipal account of boys' separation from the mother, specifically whether this was achieved by a process of repudiation or renunciation, has enormous significance for their retention of identifications with mother's care and therefore for their own capacity to care. The same processes will also affect their openness to relatedness, because it is their early relatedness to their mothers, at this stage defined by dependency, which makes them feel so vulnerable. This argument reveals boys' autonomy (in the Freudian sense; that is, a defence against the pain of premature separation from the mother) as a compromise formation; that is, a structure of personality formed for defensive purposes involving the forfeit of potentialities. This resembles Fox Keller's 'static autonomy' (see above). For many boys, the Oedipal dynamic takes place too early, too quickly and too much under threat, leaving the kind of separation that bears the marks of trauma, namely 'when the boy repudiates the identification with the mother, thus losing access to an important means of remaining in relation to her' (Benjamin 1998: 30).

Freud's account of what happens to girls tails off at the age defined by boys' Oedipal conflict, and structurally is assumed by him to be a reflection of that, as Horney (1926) noted. Ron Britton (2002) disagrees with Freud's insistence on the idea of female castration in his account of girls' Oedipal conflict (the idea that girls unconsciously experience themselves as 'castrated' and therefore need to prove that they possess a symbolic substitute for the penis). He believes that Freud 'was accurate in his description of this complex as something that can be found in the analyses of some women, but he was misguided in regarding it a part of normal female development' (Britton 2002: 109). Britton's reading of the Oedipus complex throws a different light on the child's relationship with both its parents (see Chapter 3).

Girls' experience of separation is not structured by Oedipal dynamics in the same way. Girls do often turn to the father, but not only for Oedipal reasons (see Chapter 5). Benjamin argues that girls' initial turn to the father is motivated by identificatory love (a pre-Oedipal dynamic), which enables the girl to aspire to be like the father. Freud thought that girls' turn to the father is out of object love, wanting him for what she could not have – an effect of facing gender complementarity. This established her sexuality (assuming, as Freud did, that she would become heterosexual). For boys, their love of the mother is experienced as a threat to the father, who will retaliate. But girls' love for their mother is not an Oedipal threat to the father and they perceive their destiny as becoming like her. Thus girls' separation is not inflicted so traumatically. Chodorow glimpsed this in her 1978 book but at the time, influenced as she was by the contemporary two-person emphasis in psycho-analytic thought, did not incorporate an analysis of the unconscious triangular dynamics that in psychoanalysis are understood through the idea of Oedipal conflict. She argued then that mothers pushed boys away earlier than girls, an argument that simply raises the question of why this would be the case.

Gilligan's work with adolescent North American girls suggested a later crisis in identity, which she claims is equivalent but not parallel to what boys go through much earlier (2002: 224; Gilligan et al. 1988). This is when the girls appeared to forfeit their 'voice', a part of themselves that is rooted in knowing and expressing their own desires, irrespective of patriarchal pressure. The evidence of the Harvard group emphasises the compliance that girls demonstrate when entering into relationships with boys. It makes sense to understand this evidence as a product of girls' later conflicts of establishing their gender in an environment of gender complementarity. This is like the classic Oedipal conflict inasmuch as it is structured around the issue of loss, because being a girl involves giving up what one would have as a boy. At this age, the achievement of a feminine gender identity acquires a new layer of urgency in an environment of heteronormativity, in which entering into a heterosexual relationship is the sign of successful femininity.

There are thus important similarities and differences between girls' and boys' passage into separation, differentiation and gender identity. Whereas boys have suffered their most traumatic transition at a young and excessively vulnerable age, when gender conflict and loss are horrendously mixed up with desire for their mothers, girls at adolescence are in a different phase, faced with more absolute prospects of separation like leaving home, making the transition into adult sexuality and managing their lives without parental support. Their differentiated autonomous selves are more developed and they will have a more or less sophisticated capacity to reflect on their experience (Gilligan's sample was articulate about this). Conflict that can be symbolised (despite their 'loss of voice', they are in a different position from boys at around four years old) has a less traumatic effect on subjectivity. We can suppose, therefore, that the early effect on boys of Oedipal dynamics is more severe than that on girls both early and in adolescence. Nonetheless, there is an intense conflict, evidenced in Gilligan's work and beyond, between active authenticity and the expectations of feminine passivity still current in heterosexual and gender relations, although under challenge (Phillips 2000).

If we read this later conflict through a critique of Freud's remarks on girls' passivity, as Benjamin (1998) does, it casts light on what kind of crisis girls might be experiencing in adolescence. Many have pointed out how active little girls are ('the boss of the nursery'), as would follow from maternal identifications, and so it is an important step to understand a move from activity to passivity in girls. Benjamin argues that boys face a crisis of what to do with the sexual stimulation that they perceive as emanating from the mother. The boy is not good at containing this and, through the unconscious process of projection, 'splits off the experience of being the passive, stimulated one – lodging this helplessness in the female and defining it as the feminine position' (Benjamin 1998: 30). This position, she argues, 'becomes the structural basis for the figure of the daughter, which coincides with Freud's idea of passive sexuality in the daughter and his idea of 'the Oedipal daughter's switch from being identified with the active mother to being the father's passive object' (ibid: 31).

It is worth remembering that by no means all of Gilligan's interviewees identified with feminine passivity. Because Gilligan's paradigm did not involve finding out about girls' families, we do not know if and how this coincides with their real parental relations and we know even less about their 'internal' parents. However, object relations theory suggests that the active girls retained identifications with an active mother figure. The widespread recognition that adolescence is when Oedipal conflicts are reworked within the context of post-pubertal sexuality and a further level of separation from parental care, would then be consistent with the evidence presented by the Harvard group, namely that adolescent girls become more passive in relation to their own desires and that this often happens in the context of fitting into relationships with boys (Freud's object love at a later point). However, experiencing harsh conflicts later than boys, girls have more scope for symbolising them. This corresponds to what Benjamin (1998: 33) refers to as 'tolerating the tension of opposing desires and identifications', as a part of what she calls 'postoedipal complementarity' (the complementary gender differences that follow the Oedipus complex).

Reasoning, thinking, omnipotence and care

How can this argument about boys' and girls' different encounters with loss, psychological differentiation and gender illuminate the possible gender difference in Gilligan's vignettes of the moral reasoning of Amy and Jake, two eleven-year-old children? Several decades after Gilligan's original research, it is still unclear whether and how gender difference should be claimed in explaining these different modes of reasoning. Whereas she was widely taken as showing that girls were more likely to use an ethic of care in their reasoning (and more generally were better at care, which fitted anyway with popular belief), Gilligan herself wanted to claim the ethic of care for both sexes, as part of the inherent relationality of self. However, she never justified and sustained this position theoretically.

In abstracting the principles and removing himself from the particular, Jake is engaging in what has been called instrumental reason. Alford (1989: 139) characterises this as the kind of reasoning that forces reality into categories that are then believed to be adequate to that reality in the sense that they tell us all we need to know. The idea of instrumental reason is drawn from Freud's account of the boy's Oedipal conflicts that produce moral autonomy as a defence against the pain of premature separation from the mother. In other words, instrumental reasoning is characteristic of masculinity. Freud thought of it as a positive achievement. However, following Benjamin's argument, Oedipus fosters compliance to outside authority; that is, it produces a strong superego, as a result of a traumatic separation from the mother. It does not produce a strong ego,[12] in the sense of a self structure that has internalised and owned good parts of loved others. A fragile but well-defended ego will dampen the capacity for lively identifications with others (whether these others are known, impersonal or even imaginary).

I think that this is the dynamic source of the difference between Jake and Amy. Jake's thinking is lacking in emotional connections (and in other parts, full of explosive imagery about killing). It corresponds to Bion's 'knowing about' (1962a), depleted of emotional identifications and motivated by the continued desire to control the external world (earlier, the mother), a desire that comes from retaining omnipotence as a defence against an intransigent and anxiety-provoking reality. In contrast Amy is 'learning by experience' (ibid), which is acquired through experiences of containment by a caring (m)other and through identification retains the emotional, relational and grounded characteristics of that kind of thinking. Amy is able creatively to apply what she knows about people in relationships to the ethical dilemma she is given. The questions she formulates are relevant to the way real people behave and account for their actions; the kind of questions she could only come up with by drawing on her own experience and using her identifications with the characters in the dilemma. According to my argument, above, about the different ages at which Oedipal-type dynamics impose most conflictually on boys and girls (four or five versus adolescence), Jake and Amy, both eleven years old, are on different sides of this process that threatens to deplete young people of what Gilligan calls their 'voice'.[13]

35

Here I want to be explicit about the distinction between sex differences and gender differences (a distinction that unfortunately has been lost with the dominance of a social constructionist paradigm on identity that claims that all differences are socially produced and therefore gender differences). The difference between Amy and Jake is not a sex difference: it is not a difference that distinguishes human males from human females.[14] Gilligan's data include boys who reasoned more like Amy and girls who reasoned more like Jake (Broughton 1993). Gender differences are much more complex, open-ended and unpredictable. As is detailed in Chapter 5, multiple and conflictual forces impact on how children and adolescents acquire their particular way of being a boy or girl: there are discourses and socio-economic structures, real parents (and others who are models for identification, both within and across sex) but also how fathers and mothers, men and women, are represented in unconscious fantasy (what psychoanalysis calls the 'internal' parents and other objects). There are also real biological and reproductive differences and again it is important to theorise how these are represented in unconscious fantasy.

Nonetheless, within all of the unpredictability – and despite seismic changes in gender relations – it is, I believe, possible to argue as a generalisation that currently women and men, and girls and boys, demonstrate patterns of thinking and acting in relation to others in which girls and women are more likely to use an ethic of care. Methodologically I have proceeded here by a process of theoretical extrapolation from Gilligan's two cases. Importantly, the theoretical argument, when explaining the patterning, also allows divergence from it (see below). I discuss this in detail in the context of gender development in Chapter 5. Here I take further the psychoanalytic arguments about the universal dynamics concerning the desire for control and domination in self development. Both these moves help to unsettle the dualism – which historically has been so gendered – between care and justice (see Chapter 6).

Broughton (1993) raises a further important objection about the validity of Gilligan's (and Kohlberg's) findings, namely that they are based on talk and not action and do not therefore tell us anything about people's actual ethical practices. It is indeed a legacy of the whole enlightenment rationalistic tradition that reasoning has been seen as the epitome of ethical conduct: the critique of this tradition has been captured in the single word 'phallogocentric', which quite intentionally makes the connection between reason and the word (logos), on the one hand, and masculinity (phallus) on the other. Nowhere has this been more influential than in science, which, since the seventeenth century, has developed from a principle of humanity living in tune with nature to one based on control and domination of nature (Fox Keller 1985). The kind of psychology that Gilligan was still practising at the time was likewise constrained by positivist principles (Henriques et al. 1984). However, in psychoanalysis there is a tradition of theorising thinking outside of this cognitivist paradigm, a tradition that suggests how reasoning and action are to some extent based on the same unconscious affective structures, motivated by a desire to dominate and control. Bion's theory of thinking provides a detailed account of inter-

and intra-subjective dynamics involved in development, drawing on his clinical experience.

An important theme in psychoanalytic accounts of the development of self is the struggle to give up infant omnipotence. In early infant life, relations to objects are 'wholly egocentric and omnipotent' (Segal 1979: 123); that is, they are dominated by defensive needs concerned with psychological safety and not reality. Primitive knowing is not a matter of undeveloped cognitive capacity; rather it is an emotional knowing about objects in the external world (people and things) based on an early form of communication known as projective identification.[15] This unmediated emotional knowing pivots on a single axis; whether the object is benevolent or malevolent. The object is not recognised realistically (which would require differentiation) but through projective identification. Hinshelwood emphasises that it is 'the disturbances in these states [of knowing] that lead to a manipulative attitude to the world of objects, an omnipotence to bring it into line with a more congenial "known" world' (1991: 297). When such states of mind predominate, a person's relationship to external reality will be compromised.

Klein's account of self and moral development, according to Segal, involves the child in 'a gradual abandonment of projective identification and omnipotent control, which leads to an acceptance of reality' (1979: 152). This new capacity is primarily one of recognising and tolerating the ambivalent character of that external reality (both good and bad) in its effects on one's feelings of safety and experiences of satisfaction.

For Winnicott too, omnipotence is a key feature of infancy and later manifests in people's relationship to reality. Despite the fact that the infant's experience of omnipotence is illusory, it nonetheless means that it experiences the mother as under its omnipotent control. Experiences of the external object do not impose on a passive infant, rather on one whose capacity for illusion mediates this relationship. Initially there are subjective objects; that is, objects experienced through the compelling psychological need of the infant for control, however illusory. But when an object 'is discovered to be beyond omnipotent control' (Phillips 1988: 114) a person's relationship to it must change. It becomes, in Winnicott's terms, an object, objectively perceived. The mother can eventually be an object 'out there' – separate, but sharing a reality. The corollary of this is to experience the self also as separate from the object. This move from creating 'subjective objects' to an ability to acknowledge 'objects, objectively perceived' is therefore central to my attempts to understand the capacity to face actualities, even when unpleasant. Facing reality, including its unwelcome and threatening aspects, is central to all thinking, all attempts to understand the world, and all ethical practices, including the capacity to care.

For Bion, the relinquishing of omnipotence becomes the criterion of psycho-logical development, and with it goes 'the acknowledgement of reality, internal and external' (Hinshelwood 1991: 400). The implication is that relinquishing omnipotence is a condition for the capacity to exercise objectivity.[16] A second implication is that the distinction between internal and external reality is never reliably or finally accomplished but that thinking is a result of a continuous tension between phantasy and reality.

In fact, giving up omnipotence is never secure and the desire for control remains a constant feature in adult life. Adults' sophisticated capacities for thought are shaped by this desire, as thinking is the primary channel through which we can control our experience of the external world. Bion's theory of thinking emphasises the potential pain of knowing (leading to a defensive stripping of meaning) and clarifies the defensive purposes in wishing not to know (–K). Bion distinguished between 'the aim of the lie and the aim of the truth', the difference relating to intolerance of the pain associated with feelings of frustration (Bion 1962a: 48). The relation between the subject (knower) and object (known) can be such that it '. . . no longer represents the painful emotional experience but the supposedly painless one. Such a manoeuvre is intended not to affirm but to deny reality' (Bion 1962a: 49). Bion is sceptical of the kinds of knowledge that are stripped of emotional experience, whose raison d'être is to substitute rigid control of the world that can be thought (–K) for the uncertainty of being open to new experiences through thinking (+K). This idea of pursuing the goal of a kind of knowing stripped of affect is consistent with Gilligan's comment that Jake turned a human dilemma into a maths problem. I take this to mean that Jake gained a secure sense of knowing and therefore control by imposing an abstract solution on what could be a messy human problem.[17]

Bion's description resembles the Frankfurt School's critique of 'instrumental reason' (specifically Horkheimer and Adorno); a kind of reason in which objects are defined according to 'how they may best be manipulated or controlled' (Alford 1989: 139). This too is seen as the result of a failure to transcend narcissistic omnipotence so that it is defended through symbolic activity. However, the Frankfurt School thinkers relied on Freud's original theorisation of Oedipal conflict, resulting in moral autonomy and instrumental reason (Alford 1989: 144). Here there is a conflict in their account because they are profoundly critical of the effects of instrumental reasoning and yet endorse the desirability of the Oedipal conflict. Benjamin argues, as we saw above, that they confuse the process that produces a strong superego with what produces a strong ego (1978). In Benjamin's and Alford's view, Oedipal dynamics foster compliance to outside authority. This robs the thinker of the possibility of 'concern for the object qua object' (Alford 1989: 183).

This kind of concern, which Alford links with 'reparative' as opposed to 'instrumental' reason, provides a way of thinking about an alternative to omnipotent control through thought that is linked to an ethic of care. In this mode, care or concern for the object will involve laying oneself open to the new experience and using the resources of one's mind as the instrument of learning, as free as possible of the defences against finding out something that could pose a threat to one's self and of the beliefs that form a carapace around it. In Alford's concept of reparative reasoning is contained the key to the link between thinking (and reasoning) and the capacity to care. It involves 'caritas', or care, because it does not reduce complex human problems to abstract objects, nor sacrifice their unpredictability to the need for certainty. It involves entering into the imagined scenario through an identificatory caring for the objects involved.

Alford (1989: 165) regards the example of Amy's reasoning in the Heinz dilemma as being one of 'reparative reason' because of its 'embodiment of caritas and in its rejection of single-principle solutions to complex moral problems, solutions that often fail to respect the complexity and subtlety of the people and facts involved'. Reparative reason derives from the Kleinian concept of reparation, an impulse stemming from gratitude. Reparation, for Klein, is the primary instigator of a person's moral development. It comes with recognising good and bad in the same object and facing the intensity of both our love and hate. I am suggesting that boys and girls face this task with different handicaps, which are dealt by their positions within gender difference. However, if we accept Benjamin's argument that, in favourable internal and external circumstances, boys can renounce rather than repudiate their identifications with the mother's love (see Chapter 5), then it is also possible to see how the difference between instrumental and reparative reason is not a sexed but a gendered difference. Girls too, faced with intolerable threats to fragile egos, may resort to defences against feeling and, motivated by desires to control the external world through their knowing, find a relief in instrumental reasoning.

Conclusions

Here we have an account of the gendering of the capacity to care that recognises differences both between and among boys and girls. It does not dismiss the profound (psychological, not biological) origins of these differences in early relationships with parents, but it also offers the possibility of understanding how changes in parenting practices can enhance boys' capacity to care (see Chapter 5), thus addressing the concerns originally expressed in Chodorow's early work. It maintains a balance between theorising developmental processes that apply equally to girls and boys, and those that transmit gender difference. In successful development, separation and autonomy are achieved in the context of relationality, and caring relationships are the result of successful differentiation. The other side of the developmental process is when loss and psychological trauma lead to defences against perceived threats to the self and the shoring up of omnipotence. Defensive autonomy results, but this comes from problematic separation, not separation per se.

Once defensive autonomy and instrumental reasoning are distinguished clearly from justice reasoning, the care–justice dualism is further unsettled. Justice reasoning can then be seen more neutrally as a level of abstraction that is required for some forms of understanding and action, forms that deal in large numbers rather than individuals, right up to principles based on common humanity. The consequences of this change in level with regard to the motivation for action invite us to reintroduce the question of ethical subjectivity and the capacity to care in the context of the discursive and institutional supports for putting it into practice (see Chapter 6).

I have argued that the need for separation and differentiation from the mother, or other early carer, is an essential aspect of contemporary Western self development and psychological health, but that this is not at the expense of connectedness or being in relation; rather it is necessary for it. Separation is a universal challenge in human development. I explore this in more detail in Chapter 3 through the theme of self development and the capacity to care. It is also a strongly gendered process because of the profound historical, biological and cultural links through mothering. I follow up these themes in Chapters 4 and 5. Here I have shown the need for a clear distinction between sex and gender difference and argued that differences in care and justice reasoning in Gilligan's empirical material can be theorised in terms of gender differences. This involves explaining the different challenges that boys and girls face when separating from mothers and the different ages at which loss of spontaneity in self expression are likely to take effect in Western cultures. It also involves having a theory of thinking that accounts for the effects of separation and Oedipal trauma, rather than separating reasoning from emotion.

3

INTERSUBJECTIVITY IN SELF DEVELOPMENT

Things that always love us, that is that constantly satisfy all our needs, we do not notice as such, we simply reckon them as part of our subjective ego; things which are and always have been hostile to us, we simply deny; but to those things that do not yield unconditionally to our desires, which we love because they bring us satisfaction and hate because they do not submit to us in everything, we attach special mental marks, memory-traces with the quality of objectivity and we are glad when we find them again in reality, and, when we are able to love them once more.

(Ferenczi 1926/1980: 371)

Babies don't care

In this chapter I elaborate on the psychoanalytic account of self and moral development within family dynamics, particularly the infant–mother relationship[1] that, as I have suggested, is a necessary part of understanding the capacity to care. Although this literature does not usually address the capacity to care (with the notable exception of Winnicott, who theorises the capacity for concern), it is possible to extrapolate a detailed, complex account of the emergence of an individual's capacity to care. The basis for people's social and moral being, as elucidated by recent trends in psychoanalysis, is that human beings are 'in a primary and continuing interdependency on others' (Rustin 1991: 20).

All traditions of psychoanalytic thought share the principle that conflict 'produces psychic life through the exigency of thought' (Mitchell 2003: 72) and is to a great extent outside the realm of conscious awareness. It is the principles of unconscious dynamics, conflict, intersubjectivity, body and mind as constituting subjectivity that guide the understanding of the capacity to care in this book. These characterise the infant–mother relationship (in a sense even before birth). Whether or not the mother has a distinct sense of her own self, she is now implicated in a new unit, created out of the fact of pregnancy, infantile dependence and a whole human cultural history of female reproductivity. Developmental psychoanalysis has been criticised for focusing on the baby to the exclusion of understanding the mother's position, except as object of her baby's demands. In an important sense, she is such an object, and my treatment in this chapter reflects that, while maintaining the tension between this and the mother as subject in her own right. In addition, here I concentrate on providing an account of babies' development of a capacity to care, whereas in the following chapter I shift focus to a theorisation of maternal subjectivity. In both cases, the emphasis is on the intersubjectivity of the mother–child couple, so that it is impossible to separate out analysis of one from the other.

Babies are not born with a capacity to care but they do need care. They have a capacity to communicate their internal states, and by extension their needs, to someone, usually an adult, on whom they depend absolutely for physical survival, psychological security and viability. We therefore need an account of the development of the capacity to care that starts with this non-reciprocal, asymmetrical relationship and shows the conditions under which it changes.

Herbert Marcuse, in a conversation with Jurgen Habermas shortly before his death, said 'I know wherein our most basic value judgements are rooted, in compassion, in our sense for the suffering of others' (1980: 11–12, cited in Alford 1989: 41). He draws on the Latin root of the meaning of compassion (the prefix 'with' followed by passion meaning suffering). According to Milan Kundera in *The unbearable lightness of being*, compassion also, in other European languages, has a different root where 'with' is combined with 'feeling'. He says 'this kind of compassion therefore signifies the maximal capacity of affective imagination, the art of emotional telepathy. In the hierarchy of sentiments, then, it is supreme' (cited in Gilligan *et al.* 1988: 121). Compassion and concern are linked qualities in the capacity to care (Kitwood 1990). In the last years of his life, Winnicott focused on two central issues in human experience: aloneness and concern. By concern he meant 'the fact that the individual cares, or minds and both feels and accepts responsibility' (cited in Khan 1975: xxxxvi). He saw the capacity for concern as 'a matter of health', the result of good-enough care. Its condition of emergence was 'an ego that begins to be independent of the mother's auxiliary ego' (ibid). Here again, as I have argued in Chapter 2, the importance of separation is evident. Its implications through care, compassion and concern spread throughout the field of ethics, values and morality.

In the light of critiques of the concept of 'development' in psychology (Bradley 1989, Burman 1994), some have concluded that development as a way of understanding children should be expunged. However, we need some notion of development because everybody knows that babies are not born into the world capable of giving care and that most adults achieve some sort of capacity for this, albeit not without a struggle, inconsistency and intermittent failure. So I shall avoid a 'developmentalist' account, that is, one that assumes rigid, forward development according to a preordained pattern, and focus on the struggle for learning and change. This involves addressing the very early experiences in a baby's life that illuminate a hidden, taken-for-granted, largely unconscious dimension of care. In the following chapter, I apply the concept to mothers.

What is it about babies that means they don't (can't) care? If I can illuminate – and in the process qualify – this assertion, it can help us to define care as a capacity more specifically, to rescue it from being the elusive, slippery idea that everybody recognises but that means many different things. New babies cannot imagine themselves into the other's state of mind. At the start they do not have a mind capable of enabling them to do so. One theme in my account, therefore, is the conditions for development of such a mind. Nor do babies have a sense of self, and this too is necessary. For a baby, there is no concept of a differentiated other, nor, therefore, of a self from which that other is differentiated. Babies are completely and unselfconsciously captured in the emotional states that result from the sensations that impinge upon them, from outside and from within their own bodies. So my interest in the ethical development of babies is motivated by a desire to understand how they achieve – if they achieve – the capacity to care for others (a capacity, as we shall see later, that is not far removed from the capacity for self care).

An early gesture of care

Margot Waddell (1998: 202) presents a poignant illustration of a two-year-old boy temporarily demonstrating the capacity to understand and respond to his mother's emotional state and, as a result, to exercise a capacity to care. It is a recognisable vignette: end of the day, two young, fractious children quarrelling horribly in the back of the car, an exhausted mother at the end of her tether:

> I slammed on the brakes and started banging the steering wheel and shouting at them to go away and shut up, and to leave me alone. Awful shocked silence followed. Then someone started stroking me and Carl [the two-year-old] said 'it's alright, Mummy, it's alright'.

Waddell comments that Carl could 'encourage his harassed mother with precisely those enlivening reassurances with which he had himself clearly been sustained on so many previous occasions'. This identifies the dynamic interchange of emotional states of mind over time, which means that a caring part of Carl's mother had been introjected by Carl and made his own, to the extent that he could exercise appropriate care to his mother when she needed it. This is the core process in acquiring a capacity to care. It is irreducibly relational and is not the product of conscious intentions but rather of the unwitting exchange of emotional states between the infant and carer. Clearly then we have to understand both the carer and the cared for, and how care is experienced and produced in the intersubjective space between them. Carl's response also implies that he was able to recognise where the emotional state belonged; that is, with his mother. This involved being able to differentiate the emotions from his own; again an achievement rather than something he was born with. Carl's mother commented 'That precipitated me straight back into adulthood and motherhood. I feel so guilty at the moments when I become the child and sort of force them to parent me.' She is saying that she felt it would be unfair if, at his age, Carl was burdened with caring for her when it is right for it to be the other way round. She defines being the child and the parent in these terms. So I want also to keep in mind that the relationship of care is asymmetrical and consider why this should, as a value, be the case between adults and young children.

Carl's example poses the following questions, explored further in what follows:

- In what sense is Carl exercising care?
- How has Carl learned his caring behaviour from his mother (and perhaps others)?
- What are the conditions for this learning?
- Why is it appropriate that he doesn't have to look after his mother like this all the time?

The example raises other questions: Is Carl likely to sustain this capacity through growing up? What is likely to threaten and/or facilitate it? Does it make a difference that Carl is a boy and that he's exercising care for his mother and not, say, for his father at this point? These questions, crucially but not exclusively about gender difference, will be dealt with in Chapter 5.

As a result of their immaturity at birth, babies are utterly reliant on the understanding and continuity of care provided by at least one adult. Psychologically, babies come into the world without a 'self' or 'identity' and their earliest relation with a carer is not really a relationship, which implies two individuals who relate, but a single unit (in Kleinian terminology, they are object related from birth). Melanie Klein's work provided the foundations for the object relations approach through her psychoanalytic play technique that enabled her to work with very young children and to try to understand what was going on in their inner worlds without relying on language. It is important – albeit difficult – to imagine ourselves into a newborn baby's state, who has none of the ways of symbolising and organising raw experience that adults rely on without even noticing.

According to Klein, the earliest experiences of human infants, outside time and language, are split: 'separate worlds of timeless bliss in one ideal universe of experience, and terror and persecution in another alternative universe' (Britton 1993: 38). This is an inevitable consequence of not yet having an experience of a self that continues to exist through time. If a newborn baby is hungry or has wind or is too hot or too cold, the pain of that experience is absolute. As yet there is no knowledge that someone will come 'if I wait' (there is no 'I' and correlatively no 'someone'). Being able to wait also requires having memory and therefore an idea of time. In Winnicott's words 'Until the child has collected memory material there is no room for the mother's disappearance' (1975b: 263). As a result, '. . . a baby lacks all capacity for individual survival. When left alone, his fear of dying is never far away' (Waddell 1998: 62). This does not mean dying in the adult, concept-based sense, but that 'nameless dread' (Bion 1962b: 96) of not surviving the threat of pain, which at that moment is experienced as total. Where, therefore, do we situate these early experiences? They are seen to start, predictably, in the infant–mother relationship because 'a baby's earliest reality is his mother's unconscious' (McDougall 1980: 251, cited in Aron 1996).

Three modes of organising experiences

Melanie Klein suggested that two types of mental state constitute positions from which babies' experience is organised. She called them the paranoid–schizoid and depressive positions. I recognise that these terms, and Ogden's addition of an 'autistic–contiguous' position (see below), are difficult and potentially opaque. For example, most people associate depressive with an unwelcome state linked to the diagnosis of depression, yet in Klein, it is a favourable, albeit challenging development. These positions are developmental in the sense that she saw the paranoid–schizoid position being chronologically earlier than the depressive position and also simultaneous in the sense that both continue to exist throughout life: people oscillate between a predominance of one and the other. These states are especially relevant in the context of the capacity to care because it is with the developmental move from a paranoid–schizoid to a depressive mode of experiencing that the capacity for care becomes possible. I explain this in detail below.

Following in the Kleinian tradition, Thomas Ogden has suggested that there is another mode of creating and organising psychological meaning, which he calls the autistic–contiguous mode. According to him, this mode of organising comes first of all. It is 'the most primitive mode of attributing meaning to experience', wholly pre-symbolic and based on sensory experience (1994: 140). 'An autistic shape is a "felt-shape" (Tustin 1986) consisting of the idiosyncratic sensory impressions that an object makes as it touches the surface of our skin' (Ogden 1994: 140). It is through contact with objects, soft and hard, inanimate and responding, via the skin surface and other modalities such as sound that a new-born infant receives sensory impressions and begins to organise them (this idea of contact is where the word contiguous comes in, meaning touching, adjoining, in contact). Whereas sensations on the skin surface could well be primary in organising the infant's early experience of its body in space, auditory rhythms of heartbeat and speech will help to organise the infant's experience of time, providing perhaps the earliest experiences of continuity in time. The autistic–contiguous mode of generating experience thus constitutes a kind of floor on which all other experience is built. The continuous appearance, disappearance and reappearance of the mother figure who is familiar to the baby's senses by her smell, voice tone, skin texture and gestures provides the baby with some location in time and therefore some sense of the ongoing nature of its own being: 'the infant's meaning resides primarily within the mother's psyche-soma' (Bollas 1987: 35). Put another way, the mother is still only known 'as a process linked to the infant's being and the alteration of his being' (ibid: 4). Bollas characterises this as the earliest manifestation of the self, what he calls 'the core of one's being' (1987: 60). It is an unconscious organising process; something that does not belong to the realm of self-conscious awareness. It continues to manifest throughout life as 'the unthought known' ('that which is known but not yet thought'; Bollas, 1987: 3), a domain of knowledge deriving from intimate early relationships, prior to language.

I think it is helpful to regard the autistic–contiguous position as part of every human experience, in dialectical relationship with the paranoid–schizoid and depressive modes. Its importance for understanding the capacity to care is in helping us to recognise the significance of the repeated sensory contact between the infant and those who care for it in the early phases of picking up and holding, talking, feeding, dressing and undressing, cleaning, bathing, stroking and kissing (or indeed, hitting, shaking, shouting and other forms of negative treatment). I shall develop these ideas in Chapter 5 in thinking about the baby's experience of differences among carers.

The paranoid–schizoid position describes the infant's early experiences of the separate states of bliss and terror, and how these are used in its internal world. In this state, experiences feel to be unambivalent and extreme – extremely good or extremely bad. Klein used the breast as a metaphor for these states, because getting satisfaction or not from being fed at the breast (or bottle)[2] is the first encounter with these states. The unconscious significance of good and bad objects never loses its link to the feeding state. So, for Klein, unconscious defences remain based on the model of ingesting and expelling: introjecting and projecting feelings. Basically, projection and introjection refer to the unconscious movement of mental objects, ideas or feelings, expelling them in the case of projection and incorporating them in the case of introjection. Following the pattern of the separation of good and bad experiences, according to Klein the infant begins to protect itself from threatening states by splitting into good and bad. The purpose is always the same: to protect its incipient self from threats (whether external or internal) and preserve the good where it can aid this protection.

Not only is there no such thing as time in early infantile experience, there is also no such thing as absence. If the breast is not there when the baby is hungry, it is as if a bad object (the 'bad breast') – a threat – were there. This is where love and hate[3] come in: according to Klein, both are equally fundamental in constituting the mental states of babies and adults. It is in this sense that Klein's theory 'offers a view of human beings which in an intense and unusual way assumes them to be moral in their fundamental nature' (Rustin 1991: 19). The object that provides satisfaction (the 'good breast') is loved and the object that is experienced as the source of pain and frustration (the 'bad breast') is hated. In the infant there is no distinction between the quality of the experience (satisfying, painful) and the affective response to it (love, hate).

The term 'schizoid' in paranoid–schizoid refers to this split state of bad and good. In the early position, when there is no sense of self and other in time and no grasp therefore of the reality of a given experience of good and bad, they are radically separated. The bad can be expelled by the mechanism of projection; projecting out of the feeling state of the baby and into the object that is available (the carer). The object out there that is now felt to be bad is then experienced as persecuting, hence the label of 'paranoid'.[4] Think, as an example, of the hungry baby, beside herself with overwhelming feelings, finally offered a feed and rejecting it. The breast or bottle in this state of mind bears no resemblance to the one that is welcomed in a different emotional state: for the moment, it is all bad.

There is plenty of evidence, not just of clinical origin, that paranoid–schizoid states of mind are never surmounted permanently. Bion thought of them as oscillating with depressive states of mind, regaining their hold when experiences (internal as well as external) were too threatening. He referred to this as ps←—→d. This happens because operating from a paranoid–schizoid position is an unconscious defence against unbearable anxiety and, if only temporary, can be helpful to psychological survival. Nonetheless, Klein wrote that 'if projection is predominantly hostile, real empathy and understanding of others is impaired' (Klein 1959: 252). This is because these qualities or objects have been rejected because unacceptable in oneself and so are bound to be unacceptable in the other. The capacity to care will likewise depend on the projection of hostile feelings not predominating in a given relationship.

The depressive position, which in developmental terms succeeds the paranoid–schizoid position, characterises what most people think of as a normal healthy personality. Moreover, the transition to the depressive position 'marks the birth of a reflexive historical subject' (Froggett 2002: 39). It is also a prerequisite for caring for self and others. It starts with recognising the mother, or whoever is the primary carer, as one person, who unites good and bad (satisfaction and frustration) in the same person. This begins when the infant can glimpse the constancy of the object (breast/mother), experiencing it as the same object at which hate and love have both been directed. It requires a sense of time and linking of experiences within time. As a result, the baby experiences guilt. This is because the feeling of hate involves the wish to destroy the hated object, which is also loved: it is the feeling contained in that phantasy. The phantasy of destruction is an expression of the omnipotence characteristic of the early infantile state, motivated by the wish to be in control of its sources of satisfaction, which are threateningly external to it. This creates a conflict: on one hand, a destructive urge; on the other, the need to preserve the object on whom it depends. According to Klein, even very young children fear that the outcome of their unconscious hate will be to damage or destroy the object on whom they depend: 'the feeling that the harm done to the loved object is caused by the subject's aggressive impulses I take to be the essence of guilt' (Klein 1948: 36).

This is easier to understand if we acknowledge that an infant cannot draw distinctions between destructive phantasies precipitated by hate and actual acts of destruction. The infant, under the sway of its bad feelings and associated hate, wanted to destroy the mother who is not all good, not a seamless extension of its own desires, and only now knows that this is the same mother on whom it depends for life and love. This recognition precipitates the depressive position: the affective consequence of acknowledging that good and bad exist in the same object. At this point it is easier to understand why the label depressive has negative connotations even though it is a positive development: it is because guilt is hard to face. Klein was not claiming that one is depressed in this position, but rather that it is hard to face knowledge – and continue to do so – where good and bad, love and hate, are realistically recognised as belonging to the same person or event and reparation is in order. Reality is frustrating as well as satisfying: it is only in our wishful thinking that things turn out perfect (that is, with no bad in amongst the good). Bion regarded this coming to terms with the inevitably frustrating, even threateningly painful, nature of reality as the goal of psychological development, and he did not underestimate its difficulty.

With access to the depressive position comes a different moral sensibility with care at its centre. To assuage the guilt, reparation is required. In Klein this is understood as the urge to repair the damage one has done (in phantasy as well as reality) to the loved object. Here, then, the concepts that she is developing as part of an understanding of human developmental processes involve not only moral sentiments, but ethical actions. According to Alford (1989) the paranoid–schizoid position leads to a 'talion' morality (as in 'an eye for an eye and a tooth for a tooth'), which he contrasts with the morality of the depressive position:

> A morality based not merely upon the desire to make sacrifices, in order to make reparation for phantasied acts of aggression; it is based also upon an ability to identify deeply with others, to feel connected with their fates. This is the morality of the depressive position – reparative morality, it might be called. It might also be called simply caritas.
>
> (Alford 1989: 8)

In this view, we have caritas – the expression of care and the capacity that underpins it – as the centre of the emerging self. Inextricable from the moral development aspect of achieving depressive states is the self development aspect. There is no integrated self in the paranoid–schizoid position: parts are split and fragmented. The ability to integrate the good and bad in the other/mother entails the capacity to hold those together in experience, which is the ground for an integrated self. The relative (never total) integration of the self is therefore a precondition for the capacity to care. In the following section, I shall describe how (and to what extent) a child develops an integrated sense of self out of the maelstrom of the paranoid–schizoid position. It is a process that underlines the centrality of unconscious intersubjectivity to the self.

Intersubjectivity and the learning of care

To explain why Carl could respond to his mother's distress, I also need to explain how he comes to be able to contain and tolerate it, rather than, say, become more distressed than his mother. To do this, Waddell draws on Bion's intersubjective model of learning and self development. At its simplest, this describes how the inchoate and disorganised experiences of infants become manageable in the unconscious space created for them by the mother figure. This person becomes the 'container' for the unwanted – because threatening – feelings of the baby; feelings that the baby expresses and attempts to get rid of through expelling them. Depending on what happens to those feelings there, the baby can receive them back in what

Bion called a 'detoxified' form. This permits the baby to think. It is worth quoting Waddell at length here:

> The mother's relationship to her infant is not one simply of reflecting moods and impulses, and thereby enabling the baby to get to know himself by a process of mirroring, of recognition of self-in-other, but rather one of having an actively participatory role in doing something with the projected emotions. What is being described as taking place is an unconscious processing of the baby's instinctive communications and evacuations, which can be depicted as a sort of chaos of impulse, pain and desire, in which mental and physical, self and other, are hardly distinguishable. . . . For the baby to turn the sense data of experience into his own reflexive mind, he needs a primary experience of active holding by his mother's mind.
>
> (Waddell 1998: 37)

Waddell (1998: 32) gives an everyday example of a mother thinking through her three-month-old's distress while feeding until she has succeeded in comforting him. She concludes (ibid: 39): 'this mother's capacity to hold her baby's anxiety and her own, to go on thinking in the face of puzzling and increasingly intense protest and distress, drawing on and offering her inner resources, beautifully exemplifies what Bion (1962b) called "reverie"'. She identifies various characteristics of this capacity: engaging with the distress rather than explaining it, tolerating not knowing its source, restraining herself from imposing a solution reactively ('he must have a dirty nappy'). If this experience – of being 'held' in the mother's mind – is sufficiently consistent, the baby will experience an integration of the different parts of himself and an internalised capacity of its own to 'hold' experiences.

> He will be able psychically to absorb [his mother's] mental functions, that is, to introject them. Slowly, as he learns these functions, they become built into the structure of his personality. In the end he will acquire the sense that he possesses an inner strength of his own and is not wholly and anxiously dependent on external help to hold himself together.
>
> (Waddell 1998: 33–34)

This is a useful description of the way that intersubjective processes dynamically produce subjectivity as an ongoing process. It is what we saw in the example of Carl. Clearly the (m)other's role is crucial here, because she needs to be available to and respond to the baby's emotions, rather than imposing feelings on him that belong to her or just reflecting back the baby's feelings that are as meaningless as when the baby expressed them. Bion stressed that the communication works not through cognitive understanding but through the mother receiving the emotional communication in a state of calm receptiveness (Hinshelwood 1991: 420) or what he called 'reverie'. This kind of communication precedes symbolisation and arguably under-pins symbolic forms of communication as well. Bion saw it as normal projective identification (see below and Hinshelwood 1991: 179ff). In this perspective, thought itself is dependent on an emotional container and it is unconscious intersubjective dynamics that enable the creation of a psychic space for the processing of thought. I introduced this idea in Chapter 2, exploring the consequences of not being able to think about something, not being able to face reality, because the emotions involved in that process are uncontainable, either within the mind or with the help of somebody else's mind.

The understanding of the form and effects of emotional communication is central to Kleinian and post-Kleinian theory. It is based on the principle of unconscious intersubjectivity; that is, the idea that communication routinely passes between two people without either of them necessarily being consciously aware of, or intending this. In this principle lies the seed for understanding the capacity to care: the idea that the carer can unconsciously receive emotional communications from a person in need and respond in the service of that other person. This applies to babies, who depend upon pre-symbolic communication, but it also applies to all the aspects of adult-to-adult care that are never symbolised and remain part of the 'unthought known' (Bollas 1987).

These complex dynamics of emotional communication are explored in both their positive and negative implications in the concept of identification, a concept that is helpful in understanding babies' acquisition of the contents of self. Identi-fication attempts to capture the effects on each party of the unconscious actions by both as they project and introject psychic elements and aspects of relation-ships. The radical implication of the concept is that there is no firmly established boundary separating one person from another where emotional life is concerned (which means every aspect of mental life, including, as we have seen, learning and relating):

> Freud's development of a theory of identification was a momentous step
> in understanding how the apparent boundaries of the self are actually
> permeable, how the apparently isolated subject constantly assimilates
> what is outside itself . . . the ego is not really independent and self-
> constituting, but is actually made up of the objects it assimilates.
> (Benjamin 1998: 79)

The idea of intersubjectivity thus means more than people being 'in interpersonal relation', which presupposes two people, always already separate, who relate. Intersubjectivity, in contrast, is the unconscious flowing of mental states between one person and another that constantly modifies them. 'We are constructed of dynamic, internalised relationships between self and object. In turn we externalize our inner worlds onto our outside relationships, which turn again to influence our inner organisation throughout our development as children and adults' (Scharff 1992: xviii). Here Scharff is describing the two directions that are necessary parts of identification: projection and introjection, or projective identification and introjective identification.

Introjective identification can enlarge the ego because it involves internalising an object (a relationship with an object) and identifying with it, thus altering the ego in that direction. Waddell inferred, for example, that Carl had internalised his mother's reassurances (or perhaps more precisely his relationship to these) via a process of introjective identification and so expanded his own capacities. Projective identification is, in contrast, depleting: 'projective identification is a phantasy that some part of the ego has been separated off and relocated in an external object' (Hinshelwood 1991: 320). Whether this is a useful temporary defence and/or whether it might, if repeated, have ongoing negative consequences, depends on what happens to the projection when it finds its object.

Ogden explains the importance of projective identification for the infant's capacity to think as follows: 'a process by which the infant's thoughts that cannot be thought and feelings that cannot be felt are elicited in the mother when the mother is able to make herself psychologically available to be used in this way' (1994: 44). It works as follows: 'the aspect of oneself that is in unconscious fantasy "residing" in the other person is felt to be altered in the process, and under optimal conditions is imagined to be "retrieved" in a less toxic or endangered form' (ibid). When the conditions are not optimal, projective identification involves not only the confusion of states of mind and personality parts between the projecting subject and the other, but the defensive loss of access to a reality by which to judge oneself and the other. This is when it cannot be contained, either in intrapsychic space or by finding a safe container. When these forms of projective identification become etched in to the personality and get reproduced in a succession of relationships, it has serious consequences for the self and the capacity to care realistically – accurately – for others.[5]

There are a number of ways that emotional communication can fail the baby. One is when the baby's carer is psychologically cut off from the baby's communications and so fails to respond with any vitality or recognition. This emotional absence is common enough when, for example, mothers are depressed. Alternatively, a parent might be so distraught as a result of the baby's screaming that he or she abandons the attempt to help and even shakes or hurts the baby in anxiety and loss of control that has turned aggressive. In this case, the baby experiences its own negative feelings failing to be contained but rather re-projected; not only not detoxified but amplified. Less dramatically, reacting rather than reflecting, the carer may assume that she knows what is needed and impose this on the baby, irrespective of whether this turns out to be correct. If this happens too much, the absence of trustworthy recognition confuses the baby's grasp of reality, in which case, the baby's experience will be:

> . . . of being actively misunderstood, such that a mother hostile to understanding will be experienced and taken in – a frightened self perhaps, divested of meaning because there is no 'common sense', no

experience of correspondence between the need felt and the response given. Such a baby will have more difficulty in getting to know and accept himself, as distinct from trying to accommodate to what appears to be required, or attempting to reject the projected picture. . . . Those experiences that make sense do so because they are underpinned by emotional authenticity. They are therefore the ones that can be learnt from.

(Waddell 1998: 42)

Waddell's account here illuminates a fundamental process in good care, namely that it is based on accurate understanding of the emotional expression of a need. Later, I pick up this theme using the term 'recognition'. The success or failure of this understanding is experienced by the baby through the appropriateness of the response given. Babies learn about themselves through the carer's response. They make sense of their experiences of needs, feelings and their own early agency as expressed in their attempted communication. In other words, babies need the carer to be able to contain their distress and in the process think and hopefully achieve understanding. Carers' capacity to contain and think about the other is therefore important. For example, continually plugging a baby's mouth with a dummy, or bottle or nipple when it is not hungry illustrates not thinking and not understanding. If this is repeated consistently, the baby comes to know that this is what it will get, whatever the source of distress. Rather than learn that the carer has got it wrong (this would come much later), the baby misunderstands its own feelings and needs. The baby's reliance on accurate recognition of its needs is a reminder of why the carer needs a sense of a separate self so that she does not confuse the baby's feelings with her own, even when – especially when – she is containing them.

Consistent absence of a containing and understanding presence in a child's early development therefore implies great difficulty in learning from experience; 'severe disorder of the impulse to be curious', according to Ogden (1994: 44). This affects how one experiences the difference between one's own, authentic feelings and those belonging to someone else, imposed from outside, and therefore inhibits the beginnings of an integrated self. Such failings in the early care relationship build up into what Winnicott called a false self. In my view, these are the developmental precursors of what Gilligan refers to as inauthenticity and loss of voice (Chapter 2).

The infant's self protection from its dependent vulnerability takes the shape of omnipotence; that is, it does not know its limitations. The fact of being 'held' in the psyche-soma of the mother–infant couple enables this illusion to work. Winnicott uses the example of the infant's illusion of creating the breast just when the mother produces it. The mother's active understanding of her infant's needs is thus vitally important in the early stages. It then lessens 'according to the infants' growing ability to account for failure of adaptation and to tolerate the results of frustration . . . If all goes well the infant can actually come to gain from the experience of frustration, since incomplete adaptation to need makes objects real, that is to say hated as well as loved' (Winnicott 1975b: 238).

Omnipotence is characteristic of the paranoid–schizoid mode of experience. In young babies it is the dominant mode, with the consequence that outside objects – the mother or primary carer in particular – are ruthlessly used as an extension of the baby's narcissism.[6] Use of the mother tests her to the point of destruction – in the baby's fantasy. It is when the mother survives this destruction that the baby knows that she has an independent subjectivity: his illusions are not omnipotent. If the carer does survive, this other can be seen 'in its alterity, as external – outside one's own control and yet able to have decisive impact on the self' (Benjamin 1998: 91). So, for the modification of omnipotence by reality, which is a crucial marker of the move from paranoid–schizoid to depressive relating, the mother's survival is important. Her response, not withdrawing and not striking back, teaches the infant that she can be used and survive. Gradually such experiences modify his omnipotence. Winnicott uses the term 'ruthless' to describe the infant's use of its carer, the root of which is 'ruth', meaning concern. The passage from pre-ruth (ruthlessness) to ruth is core to the development of ethical subjectivity. Carl was capable of concern on experiencing his mother's distress. In Kleinian terms, we can see Carl as having access to the depressive position in which he experiences not only concern but guilt, the feeling that he has done harm to his mother through his aggression. His words and stroking constitute an attempt to make reparation, thus also re-establishing his mother as a safe, reliable object. In the process, Carl has momentarily given up his omnipotence: he cannot control his mother's responses.

The ability to recognise that the other is outside one's control is a significant accomplishment, because omnipotence is very reassuring when one is dependent on another person, and therefore painful to give up. It is also the central task in differentiating from the mother, recognising her as a separate person, not an extension of one's own desires. As we have seen, dependency will tend towards a narcissistic and omnipotent desire to control the other, to make her an extension of one's own desires. Alford calls this paranoid–schizoid love. This kind of love can be expressed in care relationships and, on the surface, appears like dedicated care. In distinguishing between narcissistic caring and the caring that recognises the cared-for person's separate self, I am making a value judgement about good and bad care; that is, I address the question of quality of care.

Needing an adult to care for the self to develop

In the light of this account of the vicissitudes of omnipotence and concern in the development of self, how are we to understand Carl's mother's feeling that she should not have let go of her feelings when the children were quarrelling? In Bion's terms she would be used to being the 'container' for her children's affective states so that failing to do so, amplifying the negative feelings, as she feels she did (the 'hate', expressed in her wanting them to 'go away and shut up and leave me alone') would not help her children transform these into something they could contain themselves. But Bion's model in its ideal-type form refers to infants who have not yet the capacity to be self containing. Carl, at two, had an experience of it through his unconscious relationship with his mother and succeeded in containing his own distress and containing and detoxifying her distress at his and his baby sister's quarrelling.

In feeling guilty for the times when she behaves like the child and not the adult, Carl's mother may have been identifying with the well-recognised discursive position that mothers need to be perfectly good for their children (see Chapter 4). However, this implies that it is simply an erroneous feeling imposed by a patriarchal ideology. I think that it derives at least partly from mothers' (and others') identifications with their young children's needs for containment. The clinical experience available to psychoanalysts makes it clear that, if a young child is obliged routinely to 'parent' its mother, motivated by the fear that he will lose the person on whom he depends, that is a dangerously heavy burden for a budding self whose capacity for integration and containment is still only fragile and who therefore needs an adult's containment and external good objects to internalize in the continuing struggle of personality development. The implication of a model of unconscious intersubjectivity is that Carl's mother would know this through her experience of being a container for Carl's projected mental states. She would not necessarily know why, but she knows that she feels 'guilty' for reversing the containment burden. This is so basic to her experience of the implications of being the grown up in contrast to the young child that the way she finds to articulate it is by appealing to notions of adult and parent versus child states and how these are psychologically reversed when she 'becomes the child' by losing control of her negative feelings. She therefore describes the experience as 'sort of forc[ing] them to parent me . . . precipitated me straight back into adulthood and motherhood' (a choice of vocabulary that conveys the sharp and forceful quality of the dynamic). Presumably she meant by this that she brought her own feelings back under control and became again the reliable container for her children's, doing her own reparation in the process.

Not only does Winnicott see maternal hate as inevitable (and by this he does not mean inevitably to act it out), but he argued that 'hating appropriately' is integral to a child's development (see Chapter 4). Adam Phillips summarises: 'if [the child] is not hated, if what is unacceptable about him is not acknowledged, then his love and loveableness will not feel fully real to him' (1988: 89). Hate (in this example a response to unacceptable aspects of the child) enables both mother and child to acknowledge the imperfect reality of each other as different selves and act accordingly. Ferenczi, in the epigraph to this chapter, eloquently generalises this to relationships in general.

At two years old, Carl had an experience of being able to transcend his narcissism, introject and identify with the mental state of his mother and feel this accurately as belonging to her. These were the prerequisites of his ability to respond caringly. They represent a sophisticated achievement in the development of an integrated and differentiated self; one that his mother and probably others were crucial in enabling. Carl experienced his mother's 'objective and justified hate' and, accessing a depressive mode of experiencing, felt guilt and a reparative wish as evidenced by his caring gesture.

The object relations tradition of psychoanalysis takes as the fundamental principle of psychological development that the internal world is formed by the continuing exchanges between a baby's unselfconscious expressions and actions and the parental (especially maternal) response that shapes the features of the internal world. The 'objects' that make up their internal world contribute to the meaning of every encounter. It is therefore of primary importance that a baby's inner world is filled with good objects. These are derived from the baby's relationships with others, especially its early experiences of being valued. Maggie Turp argues that 'self care must surely be grounded in a sense of self-worth, in the understanding, conscious or unconscious, that one is deserving of care, that it is right that one should be treated with proper care and respect' (2004: 111). This feeling (or its lack) of deserving care derives – albeit in a manner mediated by internal fantasy – from whether others, particularly significant others, treat you as worthy of care.

This is important to my argument, first, because it suggests that experience of self worth in babies is an important basis of the capacity to care. Second, it brings into focus the intergenerational conditions for being a subject in your own right, impossible without the capacity for self care. Maternal subjectivity depends on self worth to the extent that it enables accurate recognition, encourages children to go beyond omnipotence and is also a condition of improved gender relations (Chapters 2 and 4). I have suggested that changes in Western gender relations, precipitated by and precipitating individualisation, have provided the social conditions for many women to become subjects in their own right. The developmental, intersubjective conditions – something about which individualisation theory does not inquire – are also a necessary part of the process, however. If young girls are treated with disdain, positioned as inferior and valuable only for their domestic and child care labour, their sense of self worth will be limited to this domain and compromised. In the following vignette from Turp, I show the intersubjective processes that produce self worth in a baby girl and also how these extend into the capacity to care – for others and self.

Turp uses extracts from a two-year baby observation to explore how the responses of the parents of a baby, Esther, are internalised to provide her with good internal objects that can 'serve as building blocks for her sense of self worth and thus for her future capacity for self-care' (2004: 113). The following example occurs when Esther is eight months old. When Esther starts to cry, her father looks up and says 'what happened, did you bang your head?'

> In response, Esther crawls to the window and mimes bumping her head on the window ledge. Then she puts her hand to her head. Rob says to me 'Hey look at that. She showed me what happened', and then to Esther 'That was very clever you know'. He picks her up and gives her head a rub and a kiss. Esther seems to forget the bump on her head and perks up. She rubs her nose into Rob's face in a cheeky kind of way and smiles broadly.
>
> (2004: 113)

In these pleased and proud responses, we can infer that Esther is in the process of internalising a good object as she feels pleasure at her father's pleasure in her. Likewise, the example of her father's pride in her learning to walk is internalised as Esther also experiences her self worth in the gaze of the observer: 'Each time she passes me, she turns and gives me a huge self-satisfied smile, looking thoroughly pleased with herself' (2004: 114). The word pride, which could mean a justified and positive feeling of self worth, has come to have almost exclusively negative connotations. Esther's pride in herself seems to me an example of pride having positive effects on well-being. While it has narcissistic roots, it goes on to extend into care of others.

The establishment of a caring good internal object enables Esther's caring relationships with others. At twenty-two months, on an occasion when the family has visitors:

> Esther is keen to see everybody seated and says to me in a solicitous tone, patting a particular chair, 'Maggie, you sit here'. Rob (her father) says 'Where shall I sit, Esther?' 'Here' she says, pointing to another chair. Esther brings me a crisp, then a biscuit then takes these items around to other people, saying in a questioning voice 'You like a crisp?', 'You like a biscuit?'

Turp comments (2004: 114) that Esther is 'showing considerable evidence of an internal resource that finds expression in a generosity towards others and a genuine concern for their pleasure, comfort and wellbeing'. In other words, she is manifesting the beginnings of a capacity to care, not yet reflexive.

In Turp's example of Esther, we see both self care and care for the other emerging out of the internalisation of good objects in the relationship with Esther's father (and her mother in other extracts) who convey constantly that Esther is deserving of care just by going about what she does, being who she is. Turp defines self care as 'an individual's active concern for his or her physical safety, comfort and wellbeing' (2004: 109). The active concern is the capacity that can be directed towards self or others; the difference between self care and other care is the object. If we follow through an intersubjective theorisation of the kind that I use here, namely where, psychologically speaking, others are already in me and I am in others, then the similarities between self care and other care are only to be expected. Esther is not self sacrificing as she looks after the grown-ups, but is evidently getting pleasure from her activities through her capacity to identify with them.

When I argue that self care and other care are part of the same phenomenon, rather than standing in opposition to each other, I do not mean that there is no conflict between them: there will often be practical conflict between doing something for me and for someone else. Both parties, if differentiated, have separate individual desires, which are bound often to clash. But these pleasures and desires are also interdependent. Both parties are capable, in an intersubjective third space, of being changed by the other, so that the clash can be modified by a momentary encounter that enriches both subjects. If we follow the implications of an unconscious intersubjective model of subjectivity, we will also see that these conflicts will not be simply about self and other, because there are parts of the other in the self and vice versa.

Turp's account is strongly developmental in that she is extrapolating a process of internalisation of self care through an important period when separation and differentiation[7] are in train. She describes the minutiae of connections between relationality and the experience of a distinct self, especially as this relates to bodily experiences and the role of skin in demarcating self and providing a protective boundary which, when subject to impingements, is experienced as traumatic. According to object relations theory, it is through the mother's sensitive responses to the baby's experiences that it first experiences the integrity of its own body, helped by the way her responses gather together its bodily sensations.

Turp (2002) also analyses clinical examples of self harm in adults where parents' lack of protection and failure to convey to their baby a sense of worth has led to self harm of a very physical kind. It is at the irreducible level of the body that each person is separate from every other one. From the early situation where the mother's psyche is the infant's psyche, it develops a sense of self bounded by its own skin. Here Turp is drawing on Didier Anzieu's (1985) concept of skin ego: 'a primary basic phantasmatic cover for the somato-psychic integrity of the individual' (Alizade 1999: 6). The skin designates the physical boundary between self and other: no-one else inhabits our bodies. However, the self within this body is made up of internalised good objects and the traffic of objects, good, bad and ambivalent, continues throughout life, endlessly reworking prior meanings through the collision of transferences and actualities. These realities – bodily differentiated and inter-subjective – coexist simultaneously. They thus provide the grounds for the self's capacities to differentiate and identify, also at the same time. This contributes to my developing argument that subjectivity (or self) consists of both individuality and intersubjectivity, in continuous dynamic tension.

Esther's pride and pleasure in her achievements draw not only on internalisation from her parents but from her own narcissism, or self love, and the omnipotence that is a necessary early defence. This may be a precursor to selfishness but depends on what happens to narcissism and early omnipotence in the face of reality (part of the dynamics of the depressive position). It is when narcissism gets bound to the sort of later omnipotence that is a denial of reality that others become the object of unethical attempts to control them. For Klein, although paranoid–schizoid dynamics are never completely banished, the depressive position provides an account of rising above them.

Beyond the dyad in developing the capacity to care

The psychoanalytic accounts described so far in this chapter have predominantly used a two-person model of relationship. The justification for this is that the infant's experience is so very importantly dyadic in the early months. The weakness of the two-person emphasis is that it is a result of the dominant mother–child ideology, which includes the myths surrounding motherhood, deep-seated assumptions about the gendered nature of the capacity to care and the relegation of the father's influence to the Oedipal period and beyond (four years old approximately). So, is the mother–infant relationship the full story in the development of a capacity to care?

One strand of post-Kleinian thought regards the presence of a third figure (often characterised as the father but not necessarily so) as necessary in the development of what is often called mental space. According to Kernberg: 'it is more than the relationship between self and other that is internalised to form a basic elementary structure of mind . . . the individual internalises the systems of perceived relations among others' (cited in Aron 1996: 215). In many cases, the baby is experiencing the quality of the parents' relationship and this is a quite different experience from the dyad because the baby is not directly involved. Ron Britton explains its relevance for moral development as follows:

> If the link between the parents perceived in love and hate can be tolerated in the child's mind, it provides the child with a prototype of an object relationship of a third kind in which he or she is witness and not a participant. [From this vantage point] we can also envisage ourselves being observed . . . a capacity for entertaining another point of view while retaining our own.
>
> (1998: 41–42)

Earlier in this chapter I stated that the child's ability to imagine him- or herself in the position of the other was crucial to the development of a capacity to care. I described the dyadic dynamics that lead to this – the feelings of guilt and wish for reparation that come with the depressive position – but these dynamics can be supplemented by the baby's experience of itself in the triangle formed by him- or herself and two adults. Mental space results when the triangle is translated into that baby's mind, through its capacity to identify with each of the others and not only their relationship with the baby her- or himself but – the crucial new dimension – with the relationship that does not involve the baby directly. This creates a qualitatively different point of view based on the position as outsider to a relationship. The baby's narcissism, its wish to be the centre of attention, is faced with the reality that there is a link between them that he or she is outside of. This enables an integration of first- and third-person points of view, the former being more prey to anxiety and desire and consequently to distortions of reality, and the latter being more free from these (although still the target of projections). This expansion beyond the dyad is compatible with the principle that other types of families can contribute to triangular structures, for example lesbian parents. It serves as a reminder that, when a father or other partner of the mother is on the scene, his or her direct role as a carer is not the only issue: the baby's capacity to care relies not only on the direct internalisation of care but on its witnessing of a caring relationship between its mother and her partner. We frequently read of the traumatic effects on children of experiencing parental violence, especially when visited on the young child's mother. It is hard for a child to preserve its positive identifications with either parent having witnessed such scenes, and they are therefore likely to affect his or her own capacity to care.

Ron Britton, in the Kleinian tradition, has here taken Oedipal theory in a radically different direction from Freud's emphasis on the traumatic acquisition of gender difference that I discussed in the preceding chapter. Feminists have long criticised Freud's Oedipal account, notably Judith Butler, who refers to 'the prison house of Oedipus with its heterosexist implications for gender (2004: 135). Britton's account has implications that are much more hospitable to feminist politics. It extends the application of an intersubjective perspective beyond the dyad and beyond the mother–infant pair. Moreover, the triangular dynamic does not depend on sexual difference: indeed, the adult parties in the triangle need not correspond to mothers and fathers as long as they are in an ongoing relationship with each other and the child. I return to these points in Chapter 5.

Developmental psychoanalysis has also marginalised the fact that the mother–child relationship is taking place, often not just within an adult–child triangle but with other siblings as well, who compete for attention and have their own conflicts of love and hate in relation to the new infant. In two recent books (2000, 2003), Juliet Mitchell has pointed out the systematic omission of the effects of sibling relations on the development of self in psychoanalytic theory, which tends to explain developmental dynamics too exclusively in terms of the Oedipal relationships among parents and children. Mitchell begins to reinsert sibling and other lateral relations where psychoanalytic theory has overemphasised vertical ones. Her central argument is that babies and children are traumatized when a sibling is born. This trauma (especially if it arrives on top of separation from the mother) is profound; a threat of annihilation of identity because who am I when I am no longer the baby? The child's experience of the trauma of sibling displacement means that violence is always latent and can be re-enacted in wider sibling-substitute relationships if not with actual siblings. Yet hate coexists with love. Love derives from the fact that the new baby is expected to be a replica of the current baby and therefore loved narcissistically by him or her.

Mitchell uses the idea of seriality to convey that, through sibling relationships, babies learn that they have a place in a series in which, although all are the same, as the children of parents, they are also each different. She introduces 'the law of the mother'. This:

> . . . operates both vertically between herself and her children and laterally to differentiate her children one from each other. Vertically her law decrees that children cannot procreate children. [. . .] By differentiating between her children, the mother and her law allow for the concept of seriality to be internalised [. . .] there is room for two, three, four or more. [. . .] The mother has enforced, but the lateral relationship itself instigates its own processes of managing sameness through constructing difference.
>
> (2003: 51–52)

In this argument, it is possible to see the relevance of sibling – and later lateral – relationships for the experience of self in relation to others. Siblings position the child as simultaneously same and different. The problem of theorising the relation of sameness and difference is salient in feminist debate [see, especially, Benjamin (1995)]. It also extends to political questions, such as how distributive justice can be achieved. I have already discussed (Chapter 1) how questions of subjectivity are being raised in cosmopolitanism, to address the lack of a motivational account of doing justice across the whole of common humanity. It seems to me that 'the law of the mother' would be a potent source of embedding and embodying in siblings' (and friends') subjectivity principles of justice and distributive justice in a concrete, material way that would not be subject to the criticism of their abstract, intellectual status with its separation from practice (Dobson 2006). While all being different, siblings are the same in relation to the care and justice on which they depend from parents. Equal treatment is keenly desired amongst siblings and unequal treatment, whether idiosyncratic or based on social differences such as gender[8], has deep and lasting significance.

When we understand the relational conditions for development of the capacity to care, and we concentrate on family dynamics, we should therefore consider the love and hate that is forged in relationship to siblings as well as parents. It is relevant, then, that Carl was quarrelling intensely with his baby sister, the one who had quite recently displaced him as baby in his family. Although we do not know her exact age, his sister must have been born when Carl was still dependent on his mother, creating, according to Mitchell, a distinct trauma. How he faces this new reality, how he develops or fails to develop his concern for her, will be part of his caring capacity as he grows up. Sibling relationships colour the lateral relationships of the future.

On reading this in draft form, a colleague who has two young sons provided me with an illustration of a family space within which her younger son, Rory, aged twenty-two months, expressed caring about his older brother, Liam:

> When his older brother got upset the other day, my younger son stopped what he was doing and listened to Liam crying. He looked at me, troubled for a couple of seconds. He then looked away towards the door of the room where his brother was and shouted 'Matter Liam?' and then 'Rory's here, Rory's here (he'd heard me say, 'Mummy's here, Mummy's here'). Liam was being comforted by his father and Rory then carried on with what he was doing.

My colleague commented how sibling relationships are also a resource for learning to care. Rory was troubled by his older brother's upset. This is the quality of concern or compassion, associated with the depressive position, which appeared to be a spontaneous feeling, based on identifying with his brother. He was evidently differentiated from his brother in this process, however, as he did not start to cry; indeed, once he had established that his brother was being comforted he resumed his own activities. In my colleague's description we can also see both parents' place in Rory's learning experience: Rory imitates his mother's concern and in the process uses language (his own name) to differentiate between himself and his mother. His father is also recognised as a separate caring person (separate from himself and his mother) because Rory leaves him to take responsibility for making Liam better, neither going himself nor pushing his mother to go.

The understanding of babies' development has been dominated by the paradigm of their relationships to attachment figures, usually mothers. Lately however, in a paradigm that promises to produce a social psychology of infancy, Ben Bradley and Jane Selby (2004) have inquired into babies' group communications. Bradley (2006: 1) explores the idea that 'a capacity for group relations either exists alongside or even underpins our capacity for dyadic attachment'. In practice this can be tested by seeing if babies manifest behaviour that affects two or more others at once (ibid). Indeed, this does occur: babies of about eight months (pre-verbal), seated in groups of three in baby buggies (just close enough to touch with their feet) and left alone by adults, show fascinating evidence of picking up communications from more than one other and affecting more than one other in their responses. Specifically, babies show affective responses to expressed emotions of others such as distress, interest and excitement. This evidence is an important reminder that the precursors of care are not confined to infant–adult attachment relations but exist very early in babies. Bradley and Selby conclude that such groups are not made up of dyadic relationships. It is perhaps also this potential that is actualised in capacities to care which require a differentiated sense of self and others.

Conclusions

In this chapter I have drawn on developmental psychoanalysis to build up an account of how an infant – incapable of care and concern and psychologically dominated by its helpless dependence on an adult carer for survival – begins to organise a sense of self within the psyche-soma of its mother. I have shown that this development of self is intersubjective, from early omnipotence to the capacity for concern and its expression through reparative action. However, this intersubjectivity is in dynamic relation with the child's individuality, successively grasped through processes of differentiation. The accompanying conflicts between ruthless use and care, omnipotence and reality, facing good and bad in the same object, tolerating frustrations, wanting to merge and needing to be separate – all these mean that the capacity to care is an elusive achievement, one that depends on others for its continued development.

The capacity to care (for self as well as others) is, I believe, premised on these early developments but it is never static and always provisional. The analytic principle that unconscious conflict and intersubjective dynamics underpin subjectivity suggests that this capacity will depend on the succession of settings in which the potential carer is located. As well as being suggested or discouraged by rules, norms, discourses and group processes, the transformation of the disposition into action will depend upon intrapsychic features – anxiety, desire, the conflict between love and hate – which are not cancelled out by caring identifications but coexist in potential tension with them.

The early dyadic intersubjectivity of the mother–infant couple, extended to other carer–cared-for dyads is not the whole story, however. I have extended it in three ways: first to the experience of self in triangular relationships, second to sibling relationships and third to the lateral group. These are all settings that demonstrate and develop a baby's subjectivity and complex capacities for experiencing others with concern. In describing the unconscious intersubjective dynamics between infant and mother, I have suggested the parameters for good-enough care. These are based on an accurate understanding of the emotional expression of a need through identification, symbolisation and differentiation. This principle can be extended beyond that relationship, beyond primary carers, beyond the dyad, childhood dependency and face-to-face relationships. In each such extension, the possibilities for action change but the principle does not.

4

MATERNAL SUBJECTIVITY AND THE CAPACITY TO CARE

There is no such thing as an infant, meaning of course that whenever one finds an infant one finds maternal care, and without maternal care there would be no infant.

(Winnicott 1949, cited in Khan's introduction to Winnicott 1975a: xxvii)

Whereas history has recognised maternal work almost exclusively in terms of its impact on the child, contemporary culture is beginning to articulate the mother as a subject in her own right.

(Bassin *et al.* 1994: 9)

The uniqueness of maternal subjectivity

My purpose in this chapter is to explore what it is in the experience of having a child (or children) that alters a woman's subjectivity and to consider what this has to do with the development of a capacity to care, a capacity that has been closely associated with mothers, probably in all historical periods and all places. 'Mother' is both a universal identity and one that varies markedly over time, place and situation. It is reducible to neither the natural nor the social but requires an approach that transcends both. It is an identity that is passionately felt and rigorously regulated; still experienced as women's destiny but recently subject to choice. Because becoming a mother involves huge changes that affect women's sense of themselves, it is a particularly good example of where bodily, psychological and social processes intersect. Hence my questions pose fundamental issues about how subjectivity is theorised, with consequent implications for the capacity to care.

In an attempt to transcend the dualism of natural and social explanations, I offer a psycho-social analysis of mothers', especially new mothers', experience which also complements my emphasis in Chapter 3 on babies' development of the capacity to care. Central to my account is the idea of intersubjectivity as a set of ongoing dynamic processes through which subjectivities are constantly modified. These processes originate in early infant–mother connectedness and I build on the ideas of projective identification and containment already introduced to explore the radical potential of this model for understanding maternal subjectivity and its implications for the capacity to care. I situate these universal processes in the contemporary late modern context in which Western women are enjoined to be subjects in their own right.

A colleague who had been on maternity leave came in to visit work with her first baby recently. I asked her how it felt, becoming a mother. After a long expressive pause and the shadow of a rueful grin, she simply said 'life changing'. I nodded. It was as if further words would be inadequate to the experience. Yet this transition to a mothering identity is commonplace. My interest in the development of a maternal subjectivity started when I became a mother, which I certainly experienced as life changing and self changing. How does this happen (and by extension, how can we explain what is going on when it does not happen)? I make the case that, when a woman is positioned in relation to the absolute, unconditional demands of a dependent infant, especially if that infant has been a part of her, her subjectivity is likely to be altered in lasting ways and therefore, in modified form, will extend to her other relationships.

By stipulating 'especially when that infant has been part of her', I am raising a bundle of questions about who qualifies for the term 'mother': the biological mother, any woman who stands in for her, the father, any or every carer of a child? This involves looking carefully at the differences and similarities in babies' relationships with their mothers and other carers. It also means decoupling the terms 'mother' and 'maternal care' (Winnicott, in the epigraph to this chapter, makes the same distinction) in order to ask in what ways maternal subjectivity permeates other subjectivities and extends beyond the relations of mothers and their children. This means that I also attempt to understand adult caring subjectivity more generally, which involves asking what psychoanalytic accounts of unconscious intersubjectivity have to say about adult, as well as child, psychological processes. Throughout this chapter, I am careful to make a distinction between actual mothers and maternal subjectivity, so that I can chart the ways that the subjectivities of non-mothers who care for infants and others can also be transformed by the experience, albeit with some differences. (In relation to fathers, this is a core theme of Chapter 5.)

Dualistic accounts of maternal care as natural or social have been entrenched by the contrasting political implications of these positions. While women were positioned as natural carers, put on earth for the purposes of bearing and raising children, their status as subjects in their own right was not at issue, and in some cultures is still not. The dramatic changes in Western women's status has put women's rights as individuals on the agenda and wider movements towards individualisation, extending to women, pose the question whether women should not primarily be concerned with putting themselves first (Layton 2004). With the strengthening voice of feminism (the second-wave feminism that was beginning to be heard in the 1970s), motherhood was often seen as the major obstacle to women's liberation, with the result that women were encouraged not to shackle themselves with caring responsibilities (for children or men) but rather to demonstrate autonomy and address their own rather than others' needs. Thus the binary of women's needs versus children's needs gained currency (for example, Everingham 1994). Feminist approaches to mothering have been on a seesaw, on which for a while autonomy is up and relationality down, followed by a reversal (see Chapter 2).

Is it possible to transcend this binary? Can women be good-enough mothers and still be subjects in their own right? Through theorising intersubjectivity in a way that goes beyond the individualising assumptions that I criticised via my critique of Tronto in Chapter 1, and the impasse of the literature on women's connectedness in Chapter 2, I explore a way of understanding the simultaneous dynamics of individuality and intersubjectivity that can support the argument that self differentiation and the capacity to care enhance each other, but not without tension. In this specific sense, I can conclude that what is good for her developing child or the one being cared for, can be good for the mother, or adult carer, too.

My argument, in summary, goes as follows. The mother–infant relationship is paradigmatically characteristic of the dialectical relationship between individuality and intersubjectivity, which characterises all post-infant subjectivity, but with a different accent. This is because the infantile experience of the intersubjective space shared with the mother is not expunged with the development of psychological separation and differentiation but coexists in dialectical tension with it. The demands of new babies (described in Chapter 3) ensure that a new mother is challenged to re-experience the intersubjective state of her baby in an intensified way, in parallel with whatever state of differentiation she has achieved as an adult.[1] At the same time this will involve identifying with her mother through the vestigial experience of her own infantile and child state. Thus the demands on the new mother call up a doubly intersubjective dynamic, from both sides of the mother–infant couple. The infant's self development will have to be paralleled by maternal development (Parker 1995), involving recognition of its need to differentiate. All this adds up to a picture of maternal subjectivity as unique amongst adult subjectivities.

Lisa Baraitser (2006a) discusses this uniqueness in terms of paradoxical movements between unity and fluidity. She reads Naomi Wolf's (2001) stories of mothers in the USA as containing a tone of despair about the possibility of a return to 'women's hard-won independence' (Baraitser 2006a: 218) achieved prior to childbirth. In other words, there was a common experience of losing something as well as gaining something. What was lost was more 'solid, unified, singular', and was replaced by 'something messy, interdependent and altogether more blurred' (ibid). It seems to me that individualisation therefore poses challenges to maternal subjectivity – particularly early on – because of the accentuation of this conflict. As Baraitser points out, what these women felt they lost presupposes a unitary 'I' which, according to Lacan, is a fiction. However, even if a (partial) fiction, it has powerful effects on people's subjectivity. Instead of the dualistic either/or of unity and multiplicity that has characterised the argument between modernism and postmodernism, let us start from the idea of subjectivity including both individuality and intersubjectivity in constant tension. Thomas Ogden paraphrases Winnicott's aphorism about there being no such thing as a baby (see the epigraph) in very similar terms: 'the struggle with the complexity of the dialectic of individuality and inter-subjectivity' (2001: 20). It is then possible to imagine how one or other of these two terms will dominate at different times of a person's life and in different circum-stances and social positions. Intersubjectivity is the new infant's only viable option and this demand is likely to precipitate the new mother back into it, if she is psychologically available.

If we accept this conflict, is there any way of understanding maternal subjectivity as a process that can transcend it? Or perhaps I should ask, what are women's ways of managing, and perhaps integrating, such conflict. Either way, what are its implications for capacity to care?

The impact of infantile demands

While recognising how far feminist accounts of care ethics have come in challenging the phallogocentric subject of Western philosophy and psychology and in introducing the principle of intersubjectivity into theories of subjectivity, I am critical of the residue of assumptions about the unitary rational individual that pervade many feminist accounts. I exemplified them in my critical analysis of Tronto's treatment of care in Chapter 1, showing how she remained dependent on the idea of two already separate individuals who could enter into a relation of care. There is an obvious sense in which adults are separate from others inside their own skin, but one of the themes underlying this whole book is how, at a psychological level, which is often unconscious, differentiation from others can never be taken for granted, despite the passage into separation that is the major task of psychological maturing. Early patterns of intersubjectivity originating in the infant–mother couple endure in both, as the unthought known. My intention, then, is to build an account of the capacity to care that recognises the coexistence – often full of conflict – of individuality and intersubjectivity in adults as well as children. This will help me to understand the maternal experience of being in relation to her baby (rather than the baby's experience, on which so much more work has been focused).

Drawing inspiration from Klein, Winnicott was probably the first to develop an idea of intersubjectivity which radically parted company with the idea of two interacting individuals. He located this mother–child unity in the earliest weeks when, according to his observations, mothers respond to the birth with a state of 'primary maternal preoccupation'. He had no doubt about the importance of this: 'the mother's failure to adapt in the earliest phase does not produce anything but an annihilation of the infant's self' (Winnicott 1958, cited in Khan's introduction to Winnicott 1975a: xxvi). From the baby's perspective, he described its dependence on the mother's 'psyche-soma', which refers to a time in very early life when there is no distinction possible between sensations of the body and incipient psyche. 'The word psyche here means the imaginative elaboration of somatic parts, feelings and functions, that is, of physical aliveness' (Winnicott 1949, cited in Winnicott 1975a: 244). In this period, the infant does not have a psyche-soma of its own: it has no 'unit status'.

From the mother's perspective (she who has both a relatively developed self and is wholly responsible for the intersubjective field for her new baby), Winnicott described the tension between loving and hating her baby. He suggested that 'the mother . . . hates the baby from the word go' (Winnicott 1947, cited in Winnicott 1975a: 201). He famously gives eighteen reasons why a mother hates her baby. These are often both convincingly prosaic and contain profound insights. For example, 'he is ruthless, treats her like scum, an unpaid servant, a slave' and 'he is suspicious, refuses her good food, and makes her doubt herself, but eats well with his aunt', 'the baby is an interference with her private life, a challenge to preoccupation', 'the baby at first must dominate, he must be protected from coincidences, life must unfold at the baby's rate and all this needs his mother's continuous and detailed study. For instance, she must not be anxious when holding him, etc.' (ibid). Winnicott goes on to argue that gradually the baby will benefit by the mother's partial failure to anticipate his needs, by her non-availability as an extension of his desires (see Chapter 3). In taking this position and its development, Winnicott was one of the first to make an argument for the desirability that mothers be subjects in their own right, albeit qualified as part of his developmental perspective on the infant and its changing needs.

Broadly accepting Winnicott's account (as I do) has implications for under-standing the subjectivity of the infant's primary carer. It means that struggling to meet the ruthless demands of an infant (and of course, sometimes failing) is inescapable. If women are to mother, a struggle with these conditions – which are bound to be a major assault on anyone's own wishes and desires – comes with the job. They position that person. Not within a 'discourse' of perfect mothering (although that is likely too), but within a very real set of relations, infused variously by feelings of love, hate, obligation, pride, envy and guilt, among others. Such conflict may provide opportunity for transformation (see below) but, according to Kraemer (1996), it has psychic costs that are wont to be brushed aside in idealising maternal discourses:

> The mother [in Kraemer's view] has to bear her subjectivity, not by gracefully juggling with constant tensions, but by tolerating very difficult, and largely unconscious feelings – hatred, ambivalence, failure, shame, self-hatred and remorse. This juggling exacts a price, and at times causes us to go under.
>
> (Baraitser 2006a: 221)

These dynamics alter mothers' subjectivities. It is too soon to insist that the baby modify its demands in the light of the mother's needs and desires. It cannot. They normally produce in the new mother the experience of a demand on her by the newborn baby to be provided with the care without which it cannot survive. This life, which she has created, sustained and owned just by continuing living with her pregnancy, now requires a completely different response to its care. She will experience herself as having primary responsibility for this new life even if in practice she cannot meet this responsibility. Until now, she might have prepared for this moment in phantasy and in the reality of caring for younger siblings, but as a child she has been able to expect others to share responsibility for herself and as an adult (to the extent that she has already become one) she has had to look after herself or engage in the kind of mutual care with another adult that is conditional. Having a baby of your own is different: the demand of this other, dependent life is non-negotiable. Is it any surprise that women's identity goes through a life-changing transition or that so many new mothers become depressed? I am focusing on what happens when this transition in the new mother does work to provide good-enough care and on what happens to her subjectivity in her subsequent development as a mother and a carer.

We can see this transition in terms of the challenge to provide a non-traumatic continuation of the original 'third' space, namely the mother's body. Everyone started off in such a space.[2]

In summary, there is a period in children's lives (of variable length depending on historical and cultural factors in the construction of childhood) when their ruthless narcissistic demands place terrible strain on mothers, as, in this relationship, they are getting no consideration whatsoever. To bear this is a developmental challenge for anyone. This fact is extra-discursive, although how it is lived is not. Its implications are applicable across cultures. It is a matter for empirical inquiry how babies' demands are expressed and contained and responded to in different times and place, how they change with time and with what effects.

Ruddick (1980, 1989) argues that certain realities of maternal work, namely meeting children's demands for preservation, growth and social acceptability, produce universal requirements on mothers. I am unsure whether to add emotional work to this list. Benjamin (1998: xv) thinks so: 'Maternal work is above all representing, reflecting and containing the child's mind.' On the one hand, I am suggesting that maternal care crucially involves accepting the idea that the baby can only psychologically exist within the carer's own psychological field. Specifically, I have talked about the capacity to be ruthlessly used and survive (Winnicott) and the capacity to contain and detoxify powerful projected feelings (Bion) (see Chapter 3). On the other hand, it is not difficult to point to practices and families within Western cultures where mothers' provision of care does not seem to include making themselves available emotionally. I say 'seem to' because good-enough physical care perhaps offers a certain kind of emotional containment. If this is coupled with strong containing social conventions (the role and duties of children within the family and wider social group, for example), it is likely that part of the emotional work is distributed.

If mothers' emotional work is universal, it is always also cultural, in the sense that the way mothers experience the babies' communications and give them meaning will be affected by the beliefs, practices, resources, relations and structures that constitute the setting for her mothering. However, this cultural specificity always signifies through the meanings that a carer brings with her, often unconsciously, from her unique life history and her earlier identifications (themselves of course culturally framed).[3] In any case, within a model of intersubjectivity, this means accepting the powerful and potentially positive effects of children's emotions on maternal subjectivity and vice versa. It invites mothers 'to respond creatively to another human being's helplessness' (Minsky 1998: 119).

Winnicott extended the experience of the baby's ruthlessness to both parents. He wrote of the child needing to 'test, over and over again their ability to remain good parents in spite of anything he may do to hurt or annoy them. By means of this testing he gradually convinces himself, if the parents do in fact stand the strain' (1944, cited in Phillips 1988: 67). Winnicott was of the opinion that only the child's real parents were likely to be able to provide and survive this much (Phillips ibid). Winnicott's insights here were empirically based on his work with mid-twentieth-century English families. Again it is a matter for empirical observation if similar dynamics exist elsewhere, how they vary and with what effects. Although Winnicott saw both parents being subject to their baby's ruthlessness, it does not follow that mothers, fathers and other carers are interchangeable in regard to the baby's treatment (as Winnicott notes with regard to the baby who ate well for its aunt). My own experience and observation of others has led me to believe that, as babies grow up a little, they unintentionally reserve their worst ruthlessness for their mothers (see Chapter 5).

The infant in adult subjectivity

Closely linked to psychoanalytic debates about intersubjectivity is a set of disagreements about what in later development happens to very early modes of organisation of psychic experience (notably the kind that Ogden conceptualises through his introduction of the autistic–contiguous position, Chapter 3). For example, Hans Loewald (1980), an American psychoanalyst writing in the 1960s and 1970s, and who presaged much of what is now known as relational psycho-analysis, treats as a central issue in development the continuation of early embodied modes of organisation, which he sees as irreducibly intersubjective, constituted within the field of experience of the infant–mother couple. To the extent that Freud paid attention to these, he regarded them as being obliterated by the Oedipus complex, which marked the child's entry into language and is based on prohibition and control.

In contrast to an Oedipal view, psychoanalytically informed research on language development has pushed back the boundaries of early language experience. Loewald argues that no clear-cut distinction should be made between the pre-verbal and verbal baby because the infant is 'bathed in language' from the start. Research has shown that, even in utero, babies can 'distinguish slight differences in rhythmicity, intonation, frequency variation and phonetic components of speech' (Beebe et al. 1997: 137). This somatic component of language links post-birth experience to in utero experience: new babies prefer their mother's voices (Fifer 1980). After birth, language becomes a 'global experience within the mother–child field' (S. Mitchell 2000: 8), based on elements of language such as sound and rhythm that are pre-semantic and these continue to underpin language.

As a consequence, Loewald was sceptical about the use of concepts like inter-nalisation and identification for very early processes because, to make sense, these ideas require a unit of self that has sufficiently established boundaries, separate from the mother's body. Stephen Mitchell comments 'it seems much more persuasive to assume that such early experiences are not stored as images of a clearly delineated external other but as kinaesthetic memories of experience in which self and other are undifferentiated' (2000: 22). He uses an example that goes beyond the infant's experience of the maternal body to question Klein's idea of identifying with an introject: 'my father's irritated words were not taken into me, they are me' (ibid). Mitchell is claiming that these are still a part of him, as an adult. The significance of these theoretical developments is to give early experience and its primarily embodied mode of organisation a more significant role not just in development, but in adult subjectivity. According to these American relational psychoanalysts (Loewald, S. Mitchell, Ogden, Benjamin), unconscious intersubjective dynamics continue to constitute the base on which more conscious, intentional, cognitive modes of psychic organisation rely. In Winnicott's terms, these are part of the psyche-soma, which has its origins in the mother–infant couple. In Bollas' phrase, they continue, as the 'unthought known', to have effects on subjectivity.

Ogden captures the radical nature of intersubjective dynamics in his concept of the 'third'.[4] By this he means 'the dialectical movement of subjectivity and intersubjectivity' (Ogden 1994/1999: 462), an interaction of two people at a psychic level. The third is 'a creation of the first two who are also created by it'. Ogden says (ibid) that, in his concept of the third, he is indebted to Winnicott's famous claim 'there is no such thing as a baby (apart from maternal provision)'. He qualifies, as Winnicott did, that of course there exist a mother and an infant in their physical separability but that these 'coexist in dynamic tension with the mother–infant unity' (1994/1999: 463). It is in this unity that the third has its origins. This idea of a third space in a dyadic relationship that belongs to neither of the two embodied participants has radical implications for the idea of relationality because in this third space (sometimes referred to by Ogden as an intersubjectivity) the separate subjectivities of two participants are indistinguishable. It is just not an appropriate question to ask whose feelings and ideas belong to whom (how to distinguish between the transference of the patient and the countertransference of the analyst, for example). Alford, likewise inspired by Winnicott, conceptualises relationality beyond the individual: 'the maternal is best conceptualised as that transitional space Winnicott writes about, neither self nor other, not because they are confused, but because no one has to ask' (Alford 2002: 133). The concept of the third is useful here to try to convey the idea of an area of experience that does not reduce to the individuals involved. It helps me to hold the idea of intersubjectivity and individuality in dynamic tension. Because it has its origins in the mother–child unity but also applies to adult–adult settings, it is doubly significant for understanding maternal subjectivity.

Like Ogden, Bion and Winnicott learned something about infant–mother dynamics through the transference and countertransference in their work as analysts with psychotic and borderline patients. Winnicott claimed that such patients can 'teach the analyst more about early infancy than can be learned from direct observation of infants . . . since what happens in the transference is a form of infant–mother relationship' (Winnicott 1965: 141, quoted in Rayner 1990: 131). Clearly, then, these dynamics aren't confined to the mother–baby relationship. Bion's concept of containment theorises what he regarded as the most primitive unconscious modes of communication (outside an awareness of time and outside thought) originating in the mother–child relationship (Chapter 3). He first described containment through a clinical example involving two adults:

> When the patient strove to rid himself of fears of death which were felt to be too powerful for his personality to contain he split off his fears and put them into me, the idea apparently being that if they were allowed to repose there long enough they would undergo modification by my psyche and could then be safely reintrojected.
>
> (Bion 1959: 103, quoted in Hinshelwood 1991: 247)

Bion contrasts this 'modification' with what happens when the other – mother or analyst – fails to contain the subject's fears:

> On the occasion I have in mind the patient felt . . . that I evacuated them so quickly that the feelings were not modified but had become more painful . . . he strove to force them into me with increased desperation and violence. His behaviour, isolated from the context of analysis, might have appeared to be an expression of primary aggression.
>
> (ibid)

This case example provides an illustration of projective identification as a mode of unconscious communication. In a characteristic psychoanalytic move, Bion then explores the precursors of these powerful fears that, through the transference, the patient has brought into therapy. These have their origins in the patient's relationship with his mother:

> This patient had had to deal with a mother who could not tolerate experiencing such feelings and reacted either by denying them ingress, or alternatively by becoming a prey to the anxiety which resulted from introjection of the baby's bad feelings.
>
> (ibid)

Bion's claim could be read as mother-blaming and it is worth noting that he does not here address the capacity for containment within the child's other relationships nor within the institutional and discursive surroundings of mother–child relation-ships. Nonetheless, there is good reason to accept that the patient's mother was in this demanding position, which she could not tolerate. Empirically speaking, it is usually mothers who are faced with the demands of infants whose psychological vulnerability is a feature of early human dependency. Bion is demonstrating the biographical, socially situated workings of intersubjectivity; dynamics starting, as they do for the vast majority of people, in the early relationship to our mothers and transferring to many other relationships, albeit modified by later developments. The questions that follow are to do with how being the container modifies mothers' subjectivities, who else serves as a container, for whom and how this dynamic transfers to other relationships.[5]

In this example from Bion's clinical experience, the dynamics of containment are transferred into the adult relationship with the analyst and from a woman to a man. More generally, psychoanalysis understands such transference dynamics as extending into a wide range of adult relationships, in effect being a defining characteristic of all relationships. This is an important point when I consider the extension of maternal subjectivity to other adults.

There are further implications if we accept that these early, merged, embodied experiences (primary processes) are never decisively transcended by the kinds of adult cognitive rational processes (secondary processes) that are usually assumed to characterise subjectivity and relationships. In fact, Loewald believed that 'an adult reality that has been wholly separated from infantile fantasy is a dessicated, meaningless passionless world' (1980: 30). Significantly, this adult world resembles what Freudian ego psychology and Western philosophy more generally took to be the acme of adult psychological maturity, namely the autonomous rational subject. Loewald's distinction echoes Alford's between instrumental and reparative reason and Bion's between −K and +K (Chapter 2). Yet for Loewald, it was a 'culturally valued, normative pathology'. The potentially privileged access of maternal subjectivity to this fantasy world gives mothers, and potentially others too, creative access to the world of other people. Especially for children (in whom the inter-subjective space is not offset by an experience of a differentiated self), fantasy will continue to tap into this early developmental phase as an 'ongoing mode of experience in which the customary distinctions between internal and external, self and other do not apply' (S. Mitchell 2000: 23).[6]

This radical intersubjectivity starts off in the couplet of biological mother and infant (in utero) and as a result, for both parties, will have unique significance, even when overlaid by secondary processes. Although it follows that the experience of a biological mother never completely loses these original associations (see Chapter 5), this does not imply that she is the best person to provide care. I suggest, rather, that these intersubjective capacities are best supplemented with a mother's access to a sense of herself as a person in her own right and this might be harder for her in relation to her own child than for anyone else. According to Chodorow, 'the capacities which enable mothering are also precisely those which make mothering problematic' (2002: 16). In summary, a combination of baby's and mother's bodily experiences of 'going on being'[7] means that in the early period after birth, a mother embodies the infant's experience of being and psychological survival in a way that no other adult can exactly match.

Three further implications of a psychoanalytic perspective suggest that such modes of experiencing do not stop with the biological mother–child couple, even though they start there. The first, as I have shown through Bion's clinical example above, is the dynamic, fluid nature of unconscious intersubjective processes, which means they transfer on to other relationships (and other bodies). The second is that all adult subjectivities include the potential for opening out into the intersubjective third. Third, early intersubjectivity is soon modified (although not obliterated) by the kind of separation, differentiation and symbolisation processes that I have sketched in Chapter 3, so that the baby is gaining gradual access to modes of relating more consistent with having the experience of a self that is differentiated from its primary other. (These are considered in detail in Chapter 5.) These three features, coinciding in numerous unique ways, characterise the capacity to care in adults, whether for children or other adults.

However, there is another side to this emphasis on unconscious intersubjectivity, a side that is as yet lacking in the infant but is there in the mother. The biological mother comes to the early experiences of her baby with a subjectivity that is at least partly differentiated from others. During the period of the baby's gestation, she has somehow come to acknowledge the existence of another life inside her, which at birth physically separates from her. Psychoanalysts working with pregnant women have learned about how women are accommodating – unconsciously as well as consciously – to the idea of being mothers. Joan Raphael-Leff (1993) found a great deal of evidence of this in pregnant women's dream material.[8] Of course, there is a range of psychological responses to the knowledge that one is going to bring a dependent infant into the world, and also of more or less supportive and containing settings that will affect a woman's anticipation of the event. However, the reality of that woman's primary responsibility for another life represents a huge psychological challenge, which continues after the birth. She might have felt as if the baby were an unwelcome parasite that she wanted to expel and separate from. A pregnant woman recently told me that she wanted the baby out, she wanted her body back and on no account would she breast feed. Later, after a difficult period of post-natal depression, she said that she had felt she was losing herself, that the baby wouldn't let her be herself and that she had been driven up the wall by not being able to get on with what she wanted to do.

The new mother might experience the period after birth as being continuous with before, in the sense that she still feels physically joined to her baby, not only through feeding, but through feeling its states registered in her own body and knowing them there. She might be awed by the new born's otherness (Frosh and Baraitser, unpublished). Whatever her state of mind, according to psychoanalysts, it will have effects that unwittingly communicate to the baby:

> A quarter of a century in psychoanalytic practice . . . has led me to give considerable weight to the importance of the mother's unconscious projections upon her infant in the first year of life. These influence her ways of handling and talking to the baby and her future wishes for the baby.
>
> (McDougall 1993: 240)

Images of the maternal

So far, I have purposely focused on the psychological processes that accompany new motherhood.[9] I say 'purposely' because many feminist accounts have emphasised instead the social positioning of women in patriarchal discourses of motherhood and either explicitly or implicitly attribute women's passionate connections with their children to oppressive ideologies, constraining discourses or subjectification. While it is of course important to include the influences of the outside world on how the mother experiences the new demands on her, this analysis too needs modifying with a psycho-social perspective and it is to this that I now turn.

Over human history, mothering has come to signify through the power relations to which it has been subjected; these being expressed through culturally specific practices and dominant discourses. These have been forged through the meanings of mothering in people's internal worlds, where their earliest experiences of mothering reside. As I have argued, these will be represented kinaesthetically and in phantasy.[10] Here, the 'omnipotent mother' has huge influence, a figure given little attention within dominant feminist literatures because of their emphasis on women's objective lack of power. Many currents of psychoanalysis have concurred in the idea that, because of the infant's total psychological dependence, the mother that predominates in its internal world is omnipotent; that is, has complete power:

> I believe that the premature condition in which the young of the human species are born and the fact the infant continues for a considerable period of time after birth to be totally dependent for survival on the mother or her substitutes is one of the principle explanations for the creation of an all-powerful and invading maternal imago.
>
> (Chasseguet-Smirgel, cited in Bassin *et al*. 1994: 115)

As we know from Klein, the infant's mother will be experienced as all good or all bad at various times. The fact that this mother is female has been seen to have widespread effects on culture, where there is a common conflation of woman and mother, and where the phantasy of omnipotence can turn into 'dread of engulfment' (Horney 1932): a paranoid fear of dependency. Such phantasies lead in two directions, which, although opposite, both function as defences against the threat of mother's power. First, it can lead to denigration and domination, enabling repudiation of everything she stands for in an effort to be completely separate and independent of her power. Second, it can lead to idealisation, in order to turn that all-powerful mother figure into the incarnation of good who is therefore safe. These internal phantasies are not answerable to contradictory realities in which, say, the mother is dominated by the father or is ineffectual in the wider world. There is plenty of evidence from clinical psychoanalysis (as well as from culture) that the figure of the omnipotent mother is not often thoroughly transcended in the course of development, so that adults still live with this figure in their internal worlds, with different consequences for men and women.

Kaplan, locating this phenomenon historically, asks if changes in gender relations will affect the dread of women:

> If this (modern) unconscious was an integral part of the modern nuclear family and was produced through specific culturally coded relations to the mother – does it change as new technologies alter our social relations? And if that unconscious changes, then does the mother's hitherto negatively central place in the old unconscious begin to shift?
>
> (Kaplan 1992: 218)

Chodorow and Contratto (1989) argue that the fantasy of the perfect mother is evident even in feminist writings, which imply that if 'current limitations on mothers were eliminated mothers would know naturally how to be good' (1989: 90). What psychoanalysis adds here, then, is a series of conceptual reasons why the significance of maternal care (and, by extension, other care, especially by women) will be mediated by quite specific unconscious factors to do with dependency and its effects on child–mother gendered power relations. The extensive existence of misogyny suggests to me that these factors are more or less universal, which would be consistent with the universality of women's mothering.

Phantasies of the omnipotent mother can be experienced in relation to other intimates and carers, through transference and counter-transference dynamics, although Chasseguet-Smirgel suggests that the effects of the fantasy of the omnipotent mother would be visited most powerfully upon the primary maternal figure. By this she means the biological mother if available, or one who can represent the mother, in particular if she represents the mother's body. Dinnerstein (1976: 125) drew from anthropology and philosophy to point out that 'man has magic feelings of awe and fear, sometimes disgust . . . [and] destructive rage toward all things that are mysterious, powerful, and not himself, and that woman's fertile body is the quintessential incarnation of this realm of things'. If women are routinely in receipt of such maternal transferences in a way that men are not (paternal transferences are commonly forged out of gender difference from the mother) this will affect their relationships and their subjectivities.[11] It makes it harder for mothers to exercise ordinary authority of the kind that fathers and men do, because of the fear and resistance that it meets. Likewise it resists mothers' (and women's) attempts to become subjects in their own right because of the encompassing expression of this phantasy and its influence on the idea of the perfect mother as one who gives everything.

Such unconscious fantasies have influential effects on ideologies to do with mothering and it is in the nature of their defensive paranoid–schizoid origins that they are not easily subject to modifications suggested by the real lives of mothers, both in relation to their children and to the other parts of their lives. At no time in our lives are people beyond the constant, unconscious use of splitting and other intersubjective defences against anxiety. This applies to mothers too. Hailed by cultural constructions about maternal love, mothers are at risk of splitting love and hate in their relations with their children. In Western discourses (and beyond) maternal love is usually assumed to be natural and real mothers who do not behave lovingly are consequently regarded as pathological (for example, see Coward 1997). I see this discursive production of loving mothers as partly rooted in a shared defence against the threat (to the child that each of us remains) of maternal hate. This defence against hate reproduces, and is reproduced by, existing language and discourses. Building on the recognition of how hard it is for mothers to acknowledge their hate in a culture where the idea of maternal hate is feared, split off and demonised in 'pathological' mothers, Parker (1995, 1997) points out that this makes it difficult for mothers to access ordinary hate (of the kind in Winnicott's examples, see above); that is, to acknowledge their less than loving feelings for a child, and therefore to integrate hate, with love, into ambivalence. Yet when hate is incorporated into an ambivalent whole with love, rather than being split off, it helps mothers to think about what their child needs in a realistic way.

The idealisation of maternal love defends against the reality that women who are mothers are not only mothers. Mothers may be employed, engaged in some other productive or creative venture, have relational commitments outside the family. The fact that this is not reflected in the dominant discourses on mothering is significant and requires explanation. From a psycho-social perspective, it seems likely that the dominance of objectifying discourses concerning mothers draws on the narcissistic blindness of the young child in every one of us to our mothers as anything other than an extension of our demands. Being a mother in practice must coexist with these other parts. A post-modern view of multiple fragmented selves would suggest that they simply coexist – quite possibly in tension. In talking about mothers as subjects in their own right, I am advocating a version of subjectivity that includes the issue of coherence or integration, but does not take this for granted like modernist versions of the individual. Hence there is conflict and tension involved in women's experience of maternal subjectivity.

Maternal development

Work on motherhood has been criticised for focusing on the 'initial event' and now I want to consider the ongoing effects of children's transformations on how maternal subjectivity changes in tandem with the child. If all goes well, the changes required of the mother eventuate in a capacity to care that has a history in a continuum of dependency and ruthlessness, but moves to concern. It could be conceptualised as on a continuum from subject–object to subject–subject relations. In this argument, I have drawn on Melanie Klein's description of the paranoid–schizoid position where love and hate are defensively separated – by splitting – at the cost of acknowledging reality. Winnicott too held reality to be the ally of ongoing maturational processes in developing a healthy self in babies. The growing ability to acknowledge, understand and interact with external reality produces a pressure on the infant to experience good and bad in the same object, the integration of love and hate into ambivalence. Alford (1989: 152) regards this integration as the common task 'faced by every human being'. As the baby moves towards the depressive position, it will require different things of its mother to which, hopefully, she can respond.

In terms of a model like Ruddick's, we could ask when do the child's needs change or end? At that notional point, presumably mothers would be mothers in name but not in terms of maternal care. Winnicott understands children proceeding from 'absolute dependence, rapidly changing to relative dependence, and always travelling towards, (but never reaching) independence' (1968: 90). The identificatory connections and thus the unconscious emotional work do not stop at the end of childhood, nor adolescence. I intermittently experience vestiges of my own childlike demands on my mother – who is over 80 – which are produced in the dynamic between us. Likewise I am certain that I will never cease to care about my daughter's well-being in a way that is qualitatively different from any other relationship I have (a commonplace sentiment of mothers and fathers). Additionally, though, through her teens and now in her twenties she manifests an increasing and more consistent capacity for concern about me, a concern that is the prerequisite for care. And so mutuality of a kind is achieved over time, although reciprocal care never obliterates the original mother and child positions.

Rozsika Parker (1995) introduced the idea of maternal development to challenge the exclusive emphasis on child development and to theorise mothers rather than continue in the tradition of casting them as static and empty theoretical categories to be filled by their children's needs. The inevitability of the child's development is mirrored in maternal development. This is not just an effect of positioning the mother as a passive respondent to the changing needs of the child, but can be understood through the frame of unconscious intersubjective dynamics. The child's ruthless demands place great pressure on mothers to develop out of their own childlike narcissism, but with the child's access to concern this gives way gradually to a relationship with someone who – most of the time – can imagine themselves in your position and recognise the differences between you in so doing. (My discussion of Carl in Chapter 3 provided an early illustration.) These developments are neither inevitable nor entirely stable when they are achieved. However, the maternal figure is not simply on the receiving end of these. In the intersubjective space of the third, she changes. Every developmental move (regress as well as progress) is inevitably and interminably produced, reproduced and changed, intersubjectively. As Ogden points out, the first two (in this case the mother and child) not only create but are also created by, the third.

Being a maternal subject in one's own right

Whereas the question of women as subjects in their own right revolves around equality with men and the way that girls' gendered subjectivity is formed, the question of mothers as subjects in their own right involves an additional dynamic; one that I have characterised as being part of the dynamic tension between individuality and intersubjectivity in relation to their children. As girls and women, they

77

have succeeded to a greater or lesser extent in expressing and acting upon their own wishes and desires in the context of those around them. There will already be a tension between autonomy and relatedness here, as the literatures discussed in Chapter 2 reflect, but it need not be so different from how that tension is experienced by boys and men. Lynne Layton found that over the course of a few years in her Harvard women's studies seminars the women students (largely middle-class, heterosexual and childless) were identifying with a character structure that she was describing as male defensive autonomy (as I have done in Chapter 2). She argued that 'it is possible that one psychic result of women's liberation is the kind of female psyche best suited to a male work environment, the kind based in defensive autonomy' (2004: 35). If this observation reflects a widespread cultural shift in Western cultures, it involves a move away from the relationality embraced by feminists in the 1970s and 1980s (see Chapter 2) but not necessarily a move towards subject–subject relations characterised by reciprocal care by people who are subjects in their own right.

The transition to being a mother brings in a new dynamic; one that makes salient the kind of intersubjective processes I have described in detail in this chapter. In this relation to her infant, in particular during the period of its absolute dependence, the mother is likely to be forcefully positioned by these demands. What happens to her (relatively) differentiated subjectivity? If it is characterised by defensive autonomy, that will probably put her under considerable strain. In any case, she will probably be conscious of her own wishes, but her own subjectivity will be more or less available in the unique third intersubjective space created with her baby; available to be modified. Her differentiation between her own mind and the introjections from her baby are crucial to her ability to think about what it needs, to modify and contain its projections, survive its ruthlessness and gradually provide it with a reality that alters its omnipotence and curbs its narcissism.[12] The baby needs this from her if it is to reach differentiation. According to Benjamin, false differentiation would involve imagining it could be independent without recognising the mother as an independent agent; true differentiation involves recognising this, which means that she is not under the baby's control. This in turn involves the child relinquishing its narcissism. All this depends crucially on the mother's capacity to resist being under her baby's control. Her maternal development (as the baby develops beyond omnipotence) will therefore draw on her previous access to independent subjectivity and be transformed by her maternal subjectivity as it has been, and continues to be, changed in the intersubjective space of the third.

So far in this chapter I have been focusing on a two-person dynamic; in the following chapter I reintroduce triangular and sibling relations (see also Chapter 3), which provide different forms of recognition. The parents' (or surrogate parents') relationship can offer the child examples of subject-to-subject recognition among adults who are available for identification and this acts as a resource for relating to mother as a differentiated other, in contrast to the phantasy that she is an extension of the baby's own omnipotent and ruthless requirements.

The existence of a third term (not the same thing as Ogden's third space), which enables the baby and mother to separate, has been a central plank of psychoanalytic theory. For Freud, the father was the third term. A mother's other activities also serve a similar function. Baraitser suggests a different dynamic that helps this separation, namely the mother's experience of the otherness of her child. She inquires 'how the child's otherness may function for the mother, and what the implications are for maternal love, maternal desire and ultimately maternal subjectivity' (2006b: 251). In a dialogue with Daphne de Marneffe, she draws on de Marneffe's (2004) argument that:

> . . . the mother's subjectivity neither disappears in relation to her child's developing subjectivity, nor needs to be rigidly shored up through the mother's relation to the world beyond her child. Instead her desire to relate to her child can be recuperated 'as one of her most powerful desires for herself' [Here she is quoting de Marneffe's discussion of her original piece, p. 3.]
>
> (Baraitser, 2006b: 251)

Mothers' desire, like women's desire, has not been a visible theme in the literature on motherhood. Baraitser's argument, following de Marneffe, is that a mother's desire to mother, to be in relation with, the child 'gives rise to a desiring maternal subject' (ibid). Baraitser then argues that the child's otherness can function as a third term for the mother: the child's alterity offers the mother . . . a bridge back to her self experience but via her specific relationship with the child-as-other' (Baraitser 2006b: 255). This experience is one that 'I [mother] may be able to take back as my own: a momentary experience of myself as a self, emerging out of an experience that there are always already two of us' (Baraitser 2006b: 256). This seems to me an important way of understanding how the conflicts between individuality and intersubjectivity in maternal subjectivity can be understood as possible to transcend.

All this does not preclude a mother's commitment to other activities and other relationships. These provide an impetus towards the recognition of reality for the child, as well as being alternative sources of desire. The historical and cultural circumstances of women and how they are affected by contemporary changes in gender relations will provide the setting of the mother's other relationships. Women's subordination has meant historically that mothers are treated like children in relation to their husbands (and fathers) while being wholly responsible for maternal work and care. Their independent desires will have also been suppressed. This will have shaped the identifications and the care that women can extend to children. In this setting, growing sons, for example, will probably treat their mothers as inferior through identification with the father, and in so doing compromise their move to the capacity to forge caring relationships in a subject to subject, rather than subject to object, mode.

Maternal development has implications for other relationships and other subjectivities. The capacities that have been constituted in the (good-enough) maternal relation are not stranded there but will transfer via the third space, that intersubjective space that is always on the move as people relate to each other in an infinite web of connections. Maternal development is the development of subjectivity in which capacities to care have been gradually honed in a changing relationship (or many, in the case of several children), which move through the range from complete dependence to adult interdependence. These capacities are then unconsciously available for use in relation to others. They can enhance our capacities as friends, lovers, team-members, managers, neighbours, as siblings and as sons and daughters. As they do so, they help to constitute the subjectivities of those others. For example, recognition helps the development of the other's integration and differentiation; containment helps them face formerly unbearable ideas and helps towards integration of love and hate into ambivalence; being a subject in her own right helps curb the other's omnipotence.

The extension of care and the capacities that underpin it can be seen as a model for all adult development. Importantly, equivalent capacities to care could be precipitated by other caring relationships and responsibilities, not necessarily by one's own baby. Such characteristics (albeit not theorised in this manner) have been reported in men who mother (Risman 1987). A casual lunchtime conversation with a parental couple recently revealed a mother who was wasting no time in getting away from the home in order to reassert an autonomy that she urgently needed to reclaim, and a father who remained at home for his teenage daughter to return to. He described the change in him during the months after her birth as 'I realised that I could not live without her'. Waterman (2003) argues that adoptive mothers (and others in a similar position) may go into a state of primary maternal preoccupation when their children arrive. Where adult relationships are concerned, it is important that the relationship is characterised by reciprocity in these qualities. The numerous examples where women remain in a maternal and/or a child position with adult men (notably their partners) demonstrate both the possibility of not becoming 'adult' in this way and its importance for gender equality.

The development of the capacities to care that I am collecting together under the term 'maternal subjectivity' is not guaranteed by becoming a mother, but the infant does communicate a demand for them and good-enough conditions (external and internal) make their development likely in those who are positioned to receive them. While some men find it more difficult to find a creative identification with a helpless, dependent and ruthless infant, because of the history and biography of masculinities as other than the maternal, some men can and do (see Chapter 5). By focusing on intersubjective dynamics such as these, I have been able to extend the idea of maternal subjectivity beyond natural mothers and beyond women. These dynamics extend beyond women and children also in the way that the effects of ambivalence, containment and recognition carry into any relationship. We are all better off in relationships characterised by these reciprocal capacities.

I can see two qualifications to the argument that maternal subjectivity is available to all. The first is that, as I have suggested, there are specific conditions, biological and historical, structural and psychological, that render actual mothers the most susceptible to the intersubjective dynamics within which maternal subjectivity is constituted. For example, girls do not only start adjusting to the idea of being responsible for a completely dependent infant once they are pregnant. Their identifications with their mothers extend back through their whole lives. These are acted out, for example when girls (and occasionally boys) play at looking after babies with toys and get involved in the care of younger siblings. The history of human culture reflects the link between maternity and care; a link based on women's unique (until very recently) child-bearing capacities.

The second qualification is suggested by my observation that, psychologically, it seems likely that there is a systematic difference in the extent of ruthlessness to which young children subject their real mothers, other women and fathers as primary carers. The fact that a father, or older sibling, or adoptive parent, takes up a position as primary carer in relation to a dependent infant does not necessarily entail that they are in receipt of just the same dynamics as the biological mother would have been because, in the child's phantasy, forged out of the earliest combined psyche-soma, any other person – a third term – represents difference from that original (see Chapter 5).

The intersubjective capacities that enable a person to bear the demands of others in the service of their ethical development should not be belittled as part of the critique of a gendered division of emotional labour that discriminates against women – although in many respects it has been (Folbre 1994, Gardiner 1997). Rather, we can look at this maternal capacity – or the struggle to develop it in relation to children – as a potential inherent in everyone, which can enhance all relationships. In contrast to seeing this capacity as either masochistic or lacking in autonomy, Kristeva described it as 'the slow, difficult and delightful apprenticeship in attentiveness, gentleness, forgetting oneself' (1992: 200, quoted in Minsky 1998: 119). If 'forgetting oneself' has unfortunate connotations of abnegation, I offer an interpretation that is more like Bion's idea of reverie: a temporary suspension of memory and desire, which draws on subjective resources far removed from the phallogocentric subject. This is where another kind of communication resides, a creative one rooted in identification with the other from a foundation in a differentiated and integrated subjectivity.

Conclusions

A woman's subjectivity is likely to be transformed by becoming a mother; faced with her dependent infant's unmodifiable demands for her availability to unconscious communications through projective identifications. The intersubjectivity of the third space needs to be accessible in a way that may be threatening and is likely to be in conflict with her desired autonomy, felt in terms of her own wishes. Although other people involved in caring engage the same intersubjective (identificatory) processes, which continue in all adults as the unthought known, the infant–natural-mother relationship is the prototype. The consequences of this prototype extend deeply into social arrangements through phantasies of the omnipotent mother and raise questions about the responses of gender culture to changes in the actual position of women.

Maternal subjectivity necessarily changes with children's development, separation and adult status, ideally moving to reciprocal care, and perhaps beyond to care for dependent elderly. I have argued that the capacities developed are available to enhance care in relation to others. Moreover, as maternal subjectivity is seen as a set of capacities precipitated by others' dependence and need for care and modifying both subjectivities through a third space, it does not reside solely in natural mothers or in those who parent children.

I have moved beyond the idea of a mother either as object of her child's demands or as autonomous subject in her own right, reinstating it with the analysis of a developmental process which is powered by the tensions between intersubjectivity and subjectivity. To understand what is going on in the ongoing relationship between mother and child requires a challenge to an Enlightenment idea of a bounded autonomous subject and to individualisation theory. While preserving the idea of a differentiated and integrated individuality, this subjectivity is constantly available to be modified by intersubjective dynamics in the third. The idea of a third, intersubjective space, beyond one's separate self but continuously modifying it and the other, has helped me keep in view both the intersubjectivity of the mother–infant couple (and its later manifestations in that and other relationships) and the mother's (and later also the child's) individuality consisting of different, sometimes opposing wishes and characteristics.[13] The resulting dynamic tension in any caring relationship is not only the source of conflict, frustration and occasional breakdown, but also a creative source of change and the crucible of the capacity to care.

5

THE GENDER OF PARENTING, THE GENDER OF CARE

The shift to 'parenting'

In the preceding chapters of this book, I have been building a theoretical account of the capacity to care: first, by considering the available literatures, their useful leads and their dead-ends; second, by using a psychoanalysis emphasising unconscious intersubjectivity to understand identifications in self formation; and third, by focusing on how these theoretical tools cast light on maternal subjectivity as it is expressed in the capacity to care for dependent others, particularly babies.

In this chapter I am taking fathering as one specific instance of the capacity to care – a currently salient one. Is it different from mothering: how, when and why? When fathers are primary carers of their children, do they mother? Do they father? Do they do both? What has this got to do with their sex, their gender, their role in procreation and the structure of the parenting set up? Is there, or could there be, a gender neutral set of practices called parenting? As a way to address these complicated and contentious questions, I start by considering the recent conversion (in the UK and other Western nations) to the word 'parenting' where historically 'mothering' would have been the term in use.

Changes in gender relations are affecting parenting and, in Western countries, some fathers are taking on primary care roles with their children while, for example, the mother is in full-time employment. Western women's movement into paid work in significant numbers, coupled with the influence of feminism, has meant the spread of a principle that fathers should be involved in parenting beyond their traditional breadwinner roles, even to being the primary caretakers of infants and young children. The adoption of the term 'parent', in the position where until recently 'mother' was, signifies this huge and important ideological shift: it claims, in its gender neutrality, that the sex (and gender) of this carer is unimportant, even irrelevant. The successful young career woman profiled in the article I mentioned at the beginning of this book used the new parenting discourse when she contrasted women's and men's unequal parenting leave and accused it of being 'intrinsically discriminatory' (the *Observer* 26 March 2006: 9). In contrast, I have argued in the previous chapter that mothers and fathers cannot fill identical positions in early childcare.

Sociological and social psychological viewpoints lead easily to the career woman's conclusion because they are based on the claim that gender differences (in the capacity to care for young children) are socially produced, so that, in the context of changes in the gendered division of labour, fathers can and should fulfil primary parenting and associated domestic roles. These have, according to most feminist discourses, served to keep women subordinated. Some men have embraced this idea with enthusiasm, but the larger pattern has not changed greatly (for example, few men take it up even in Scandinavia, where provision for paternal leave from employment is very good). Although this no doubt has a lot to do with men's and women's relative earning capacities, it also is influenced by many women's wishes to be closely involved in their young children's care.[1]

However, my concern here is not with numerical patterns but with what is required of the primary carer and, given that this has everywhere been gendered female until now, how women and men achieve it. Specifically, I ask what aspects of fathers' gendered formation might lead to differences in how they care. Under what past and present conditions will a father, faced with responsibility for the uncompromising dependency and vulnerability of the infant, be precipitated out of his remaining narcissism? This is a transition that conventional 'semi-detached' fathers have not needed to go through and it is likely that this difference contributes to the commonly perceived difference in many mothers' and fathers' capacity to care. However, influences on the capacity to care begin well before that and will interact with later events.

A psycho-social approach

Socialisation and learning theories assume that changes in the external world, in this case in gender relations and positions, will be reflected in an unproblematic way in gendered subjectivities. It will be apparent by now that this is not my view. The inner world is particularly salient during early development, while babies are still struggling to differentiate themselves from the others on whom they have depended (a struggle that is also characteristic of adolescence, on a different terrain). This is why a developmental perspective is necessary to address my question about whether there is a gender to parenting.

Social theories of all kinds point to the importance for early gender development of gender differentiation in the outside world, especially when it concerns the parents. However, even if qualities of the real family act in the direction of dissolving traditional gender differences, this does not guarantee that a child will grow up associating care with both sexes: 'Even in . . . families that do not reproduce [traditional gender divisions], we can often observe the creation of a fantasy father-hero who represents the link to the exciting outside and assumes the role of standing for separation, freedom and desire' (Benjamin 1995: 121). It seems that, at various points in their development, children create gender difference even when not exposed to its stereotypical features in their available identificatory figures. Take the commonly cited example of the child, boy or girl, of about four, whose mother is a doctor, who insists that women can't be doctors and allocates parts in the imaginary play accordingly. This kind of evidence encourages me to take into account children's internal worlds; the desires and anxieties that (re)produce gender splitting against the evidence of experience. In what follows, I shall elaborate how the internal phantasy life of boys and girls and mothers and fathers will exercise a constant creative influence on experience so that gendered subjectivity and the capacity to care can never be simply read off external changes in gender relations.

At a psychic level, this adds up to an account of a self made up of multiple parts in constant dynamic tension. Biological and social differences both constitute important influences in this picture, but these influences are indirect and open-ended, refracted endlessly through the lens of meaning as it is achieved in the conflictual and often hidden realm of the psyche. Whereas bodily parts are relatively easy to define in terms of discrete individuals, psychic parts are not so clearly the property of single individuals, but variously co-inhabit and are exchanged by people, unconsciously, in the course of their daily lives. One feature of selves that is built up in this unconsciously intersubjective way is the capacity to care, and I have emphasised this throughout as the prime characteristic of moral subjectivity and of ethical relating.

I have emphasised that the core of early maternal care lies in the combination of individuality and receptivity to the baby's state through introjective identification, changing in the service of a child's self development and separation. This goes beyond an exclusively subject–object view to include a subject–subject one (Benjamin 1998), in which the other does more than mirror the baby's mood but rather is changed by it, thus transforming its mental state and providing an experience that is different from the baby's intrapsychic world, less paranoid, more grounded in reality. I argued that the development of a differentiated self, who could recognise the other as a subject in her own right, was an essential precondition for the capacity to care. To the extent that narcissism and omnipotence continue to be dominant strands in an adult's personality, their capacity to care accurately will be compromised.

Children's experience of their parents is the product of a constant encounter between the external world and their internal world where it is mediated by the psychic processes triggered by desire and anxiety. So I try to bear in mind the constant dynamic tension between the real and phantasy parents (external and internal) in children's experience.[2] Boys' and girls' gendered self development is affected by identifications with both their parents differently in every phase, as well as by the parents' relationship and the parents' identifications with their own parents and their sons and daughters. The children's own way of parenting and their own later capacity to care will be affected in complex ways by an amalgam of all these.

This approach provides a psycho-social perspective on change and continuity. Given the complexity of these psycho-social processes, how can we expect changes in parenting arrangements to affect gendered subjectivity in the next generation? Will changing gendered subjectivity have effects on men's and women's capacity to care? I have argued that a person's capacity to care owes a great deal to their relationship with primary carers when they were children and also stressed the mutative quality of maternal subjectivity, arguing that in principle this position is open to different adults. What features of boys' growing up might be affecting their caring capacities as fathers? Will this affect how they respond when faced with a baby requiring primary maternal care?

Developmental challenges to a young boy's capacity to care

In Chapter 3, I used the example of Carl and argued that, at age two, he demonstrated his incipient capacity to care for his mother when she was at the end of her tether. I deferred the question of whether the fact that Carl was a boy would make any difference to what happened to this unfolding capacity. Boys' and girls' development of a gendered self goes through different phases[3] and contemporary theory views this 'as a relational process involving identification and separation issues' (Benjamin 1995: 115). Unlike in Freudian psychoanalysis, in which gender issues are precipitated by Oedipal conflict from about the fourth year, in this view they start much earlier in what is often known as the separation–individuation phase (Mahler 1968, First 1988), in which the conflicts around independence and dependence are central.

Carl had introjected his mother's reassurances during his relationship with her, and was temporarily able to draw on that capacity within himself, clearly enough differentiated, or separated, from his mother at that moment to be able to distinguish between her needs and his own. However, at age two, Carl has not reached a phase of development in which he is self-consciously establishing a gender for himself. He is still 'overinclusive' (Fast 1984, Benjamin 1995); that is, he believes (as girls of his age do too) that he can be and have everything. As applied to sex and gender this means, for example, that he can without difficulty imagine himself as having a penis and a nipple that gives milk, and as able to grow a baby in his tummy. The significance of this position is that he has not yet had to come to terms with loss of potentialities for himself; the facts of sexual difference that reality will confront him with, namely that if he is a boy, he can grow up to be a man but not a woman as well. This psychological challenge will impinge on his capacity to care.

Use of the categories boy and girl here are problematic in the context of feminist post-modernism's deconstruction of fixed gender categories, which insists that the lived experience of identities is more fluid than the labels can do justice to. The idea of 'overinclusiveness' recognises this fluidity, the excess that resists gender binaries and does not fit easily into the restrictive categories of boy and girl that imply a fixed biological base. Nevertheless, the 'reality' I am talking about is both a social and a biological one (the marks of sexual difference on which Freud built his theorisation of gender are biological and clear cut in the vast majority of individuals). The effect is still to produce settings that, to a greater or lesser extent, constrain boys and girls to fit into polarised gender categories; and, although boys and girls might resist and transgress them, these constraints have subjectifying effects.

Much has been made of girls' penis envy when they confront the fact that they are not boys but girls, and it is now widely acknowledged that girls did (in Freud's time) and still often do, have to face the severe constraints on their power and freedom that being a girl and growing up to be a woman entailed. Women psychoanalysts have also pointed out that boys lose something very valuable as well: the capacity to bear and nurture babies ('womb envy' as Karen Horney labelled it). In other words, both girls and boys have to come to terms with loss and this begins, it is now widely believed, while issues of separation from the primary carer are keen and so still causing conflict and anguish. The coincidence of these challenges is important for gender development. The questions raised include asking what is lost and retained (for boys and girls) and how the loss is accomplished.

Depending on how Carl is confronted with these developmental challenges, his empathic caring for his mother, and by extension others, could eventually survive much strengthened, or be crushed, or something in between. Based on contemporary theories of gender development, it is possible to trace many possible pathways through likely events and relationships in the life of someone like Carl (in reality an infinite number, of course, because each event in a child's life will have unique meanings that carry through into other conflicts). Here, then, I shall trace the main pathways. First, I shall try to convey what is at stake for boys in the processes of loss, separation and becoming a boy.

Every baby begins in helpless dependency on the mother from whom they must separate. Separation is neither a sudden achievement nor a smooth process. In the boy's case, it will interact with coming to terms with the loss of the potential characteristics that as a boy he cannot be or become. These are embodied in his mother on whom he has been totally dependent. In the boy's mind, sexual and gender characteristics will be inextricably intermingled. Breasts, for example, will powerfully symbolise what he receives (and/or does not receive) from his mother: nurturance, caring, holding; all as one. His identifications with his mother, which until this point have not been constrained by knowledge of his own gender and the lack and loss this entails, now become problematic. Is he going to have to give up everything that he cherishes of his mother in order to grow up like a boy? Has he come to terms with the frustrations and satisfactions that both emanate from the same mother? This is another way of asking whether, in Kleinian terms, he is functioning in the depressive position, with all the implications for self development that I considered in Chapter 3. Can he, at least part of the time, see his mother as a separate entity, a subject in her own right, and not just an extension of his own wishes? Does his real mother recognise his growing desires and capacities for independence as well as continue to be dependable? Does his father treat his mother with respect as a subject in her own right or does he subject her to his domination? In these questions the intrapsychic and the intersubjective collide. Such factors will influence the boy's identifications with her, in the course of facing the reality of what it is to be a boy. They will help to decide how a boy will live the reality of his sex, which means how he will experience and practise his gendered subjectivity.

Benjamin's (1995) concepts of repudiation and renunciation are useful here. With them, we can ask whether a boy like Carl will repudiate or renounce his mother; that is, whether he will defensively reject the aspects of her that he experiences as unattainable because they are exclusively associated with the feminine or whether he will realistically give up aspects of her he cannot be and preserve those he can. Repudiation, in Kleinian terms, involves paranoid–schizoid functioning, which effects a splitting between what is masculine and feminine and a (r)ejection of the feminine. In renunciation, by contrast, he is functioning in the depressive position, which means being able to hold the good and bad parts of the masculine and feminine in himself and the other and so permit identifications with a mother's caring. In repudiation mode, through defensive projection of a denigrated feminine, he would deplete himself of his mother's capacity to care. It has been widely accepted that these are not stable positions but rather potential modes of organisation of experience, which oscillate depending upon current anxieties and realities as well as the build-up of meaning during a whole life history.

Imagine a concrete scenario in which Carl is working out his relationship to the threat of losing the caring parts that are identified with his mother by playing at being mother by caring for dolls. It will matter whether either or both of his parents is comfortable with this and can join this imaginary world. At his age, it will particularly matter if his father can do so, thereby recognising this aspect of Carl and making it easier to access as part of his identifications as a boy. If, for example, his father is actually performing that 'maternal' role routinely with Carl's sister, who is still a baby (and if he did and still does perform it with Carl himself), then Carl's identificatory access to maternal caring will be further facilitated because it will not be experienced as exclusively belonging to the sex that he is not. Although they are mediated in the child's phantasies, the real parents do matter: the less polarised the gender order, the less is lost with the discovery of the either/or of gender difference.

Beyond the parent–child dyad

The arrival of a younger sibling will also change a child's relationship to mother. Juliet Mitchell (2000) criticises psychoanalysis for concentrating on the vertical, generational relationship at the expense of understanding the influence of lateral, initially sibling, relationships. With regard to Carl's capacity to hold on to his identificatory love for his mother while he struggles with the loss of having to be a boy, this enables us to take into account that the mother he has to give up is also the mother who has given birth to a sibling (it was Carl and his younger sibling's quarrel in the car that proved too much for that mother to contain). The mother may be hated for this too, in addition to 'the primary hatred [which] is against the one person who stands in one's place . . . the sibling' (J. Mitchell 2000: 129). Can Carl still identify with the capacity to care when that is experienced by him as part of a relationship in which he has been displaced? In Carl's imagined case, with a younger female sibling, it is relevant how the parents' actual care divides up. For example, when both parents are available, is the younger always looked after by the mother and the older (boy) by the father? If this is a rigid arrangement, so that the boy experiences himself as having no choice between the parents, he may have to disown his babyish wishes, probably projecting them into his younger sibling and hating them there. It is common for Oedipal boys in conflict over their babyish wishes for their mothers to label all babies as 'she' and express disgust for everything to do with babies and their care as girlish. In this way they repudiate their wishes for dependency and care, having gendered them as other and inferior.

Let us further suppose that Carl has a father who works full time yet who is around and emotionally available the rest of the time.[4] The father figure will have a phantasy dimension in Carl's internal world that does not faithfully reflect the real father. This internal representation will be 'refracted through the conflicts that are currently dominant in the child's psyche' (Benjamin 1995: 119). At around age three and four, it is common for boys to hero-worship their fathers and, empirically speaking, it does seem as if boys (and girls as we shall see in a minute) turn to the father for something different from what the mother provides. This something has been characterised as in contrast to the holding or containing of the mother, something more like excitement and the activity associated with the wider world.

Psychoanalysis thus tends to claim that the father, in contrast to the mother, can help the internalisation of a sense of separateness. If and why this should be so is a useful example of the different implications of analyses that have an emphasis on the current real relations that the child experiences with his parents or an emphasis on the way real relations are transformed through the successive psychic experiences making up a life history which modify the experience of the parents in the internal world of the child. The 'real relations' analysis would look at the actual division of labour in a given family around the world of paid work outside the home and the work of domestic reproduction and care within and around the home. If the gender roles were reversed, this would lead to a set of identifications that made it easier for boys to care and, later, to parent and girls to prioritise the wider world and, later, employment.

My emphasis on the effects of the early combined psyche-soma suggests that later experience of the mother is always tinged with the early experience of the mother not being other but part of the baby. In this sense, rather than the father being the second object (the second thing that is experienced as being outside the infant), he can 'more properly be described as the first object which comes to the child from the external world' (Gaddini 1976: 398, cited in Target and Fonagy 2002: 50). If one accepts this argument, the claim that the father represents separateness in a way that the mother will never do becomes plausible. It fits with the emphasis on the need for children to separate from their mothers in a way that they never have to separate from their fathers. This is why Winnicott makes a fundamental distinction between maternal and paternal; one that I can use to address the question of whether fathers mother or whether they father, or both. He claims that fathers can achieve good-enough mothering. However, he adds: 'fathers must allow me to use the term maternal to describe the total attitude to babies and their care. The term paternal must necessarily come a little later than the maternal'

(Winnicott 1971: 191). Perhaps we can conclude that, while fathers can perform the maternal and paternal functions (and mothers both these functions too), in the internal world of the child, these will never be entirely interchangeable as long as the infant is born out of the mother's body.

The boy's attempts to come to terms with the gender that appears to be demanded by his sex make it likely that he will be seeking, albeit ambivalently, for positive identifications with his father. Benjamin (1995) calls this identificatory love. Consistent with her position of holding on to the tension of the intra-psychic and intersubjective, she reminds us that the real father (or mother) needs to respond positively to a child's identifications. Will his father be able to recognise him for what he really is? The father's identifications with his son will come into play here. For example, in the film *Billy Elliott*, the father, a coal miner in the North of England, wanted Billy to learn to box, as he had done. It symbolised the masculine hardness that the father wanted for himself and his son. He was disgusted when Billy wanted to learn to dance, and Billy had to rely on identifications with his dead mother to pursue his desire to do so. His father could not recognise either Billy's desire or his massive talent, or indeed the masculine prowess (muscle, stamina, strength) that was a part of Billy's skill. In terms of the concept of projective identification, we can say that Billy's father split off his unacceptable ('feminine') parts and projected them out. In his masculine identifications with his son, he was only prepared to recognise the remaining parts (for example, the boxer). When Billy started learning to dance, the rejected feminine parts were projected on to him by his father, where they were then identified as belonging, and repudiated there.

There is at least one more influential facet of the immediate family dynamics that will already have affected Carl's internal world and will continue to interact with it, namely the character of his parents' relationship (so that 'who cares for me' expands to 'who cares for whom'). Who does the holding, containing part in the parents' relationship? Who expresses the active, desiring parts? Are these split, or do they move fluidly between the two parents in different situations? Does the presence of the father threaten the mother's availability for the child or support it? Perhaps the father is jealous of the mother's love of the son and unconsciously intrudes to spoil what he wants to keep for himself. Perhaps, when the son or daughter turns to the father, mother is jealous and interferes. Perhaps he competes with her for the son's love and if so, on what territory (meal times, the parental bed)? Again these real aspects of the parents' relationship (including the way their own conflictual inner worlds are played out in their relationship) will be altered by the image of the parental relationship in the young child's mind. Psychoanalysis has investigated this area through Freud's theorisation of the primal scene and Klein's concept of the combined parent figure. As with any other figure of phantasy, the current and predominant mental state of that person (in Kleinian terms paranoid–schizoid or depressive) will affect the qualities of the internalised parental relationship.

Abelin (1980) claims that it is not until about eighteen months that a toddler begins to notice the existence of the parental couple (cited in Etchegoyen 2002:

31). This is not only traumatic, in the Freudian sense of precipitating rivalry and – in the boy – fear, it can also help to organise experience. Essentially, the challenge is to 'tolerate the link between two people they desire and which excludes them' (Marks 2002: 95). This is the task for all three parties and not just the baby (ibid). If the father cannot do it, the baby will find it harder. For the baby, the depressive solution involves accepting the reality of the parental couple and working this through in relation to both parents. Abelin (1975) reconstructs a scenario whereby a child of about one year old, newly facing the triangular situation and therefore noticing the father and mother relating to each other, feels left out. Prior to this, in dyadic mode, he or she has experienced self only in relation to another. Now, temporarily excluded, he experiences himself by imagining him or her self in the place of one of the others, probably the father because of an identification with the one who wants the mother: 'there must be an I like him wanting her', is how Abelin puts it. He suggests that in this way the child first sees himself (Marks 2002: 103). Likewise Britton, as we have seen (Chapter 3), argues that it is within the triangular space of the mother–father–child relationship that the child can achieve self reflection because, of the three links that form the triangle, one excludes the baby. It therefore witnesses the relationship from the outside. Again this is seen as a crucial aspect of the developing self.

Target and Fonagy suggest that it is not the presence of the father that is crucial here so much as whether 'a child can envisage a relationship between two other emotionally significant figures' (2002: 54). For this it is important that the father (or other who takes the position of having a sexual relationship with the mother) is available through the mother's mind. To complicate matters, the mother's relation to the father will be influenced by her internal relationship with her own father and so a three-generational dynamic will be having its effects. Here in the mother's mind is where the baby first experiences the father's significance[5] and it is on this that the baby will work his or her own phantasies and so the intergenerational chain is perpetuated; the chain that helps to explain the continuity in family relationships:

> In turn, the experience of father is influenced by not only the actual father and actual parental couple but also by the mother and father in the individual mother's mind, and this itself will be a consequence of the mother's own experience of the father and parental couple in her mother's mind and so on, back through the generations.
>
> (Marks 2002: 95)

Different bodies and their significance

In Chapter 4, I discussed the effect of women's biological role in procreation from the perspective of both mother and infant, focusing on the psychological significance of the mother's body originating before birth. This early bond can go some way to explaining why some mothers feel that they just know what their babies need. This is likely to leave fathers feeling helpless and excluded, with the consequence that they withdraw from the scene and, rather than learn enough to be sensitive to the new baby's state, continue to be out of touch. In this effect, the new mother's early, if ambivalent, experience of oneness with her infant when it was in her womb has ongoing consequences, particularly if combined with a defensive response from the other parent (who is not necessarily the biological father). In practice, this means that fathers rarely feel primarily responsible for the dependent infant in the way that almost all mothers do (whether they meet this demand successfully or not).

The biological mother has another embodied resource if she is breast feeding, one that goes beyond the satisfaction of hunger. When things are going right, it contains everything that the baby needs for security, familiarity and satisfaction (skin against warm, soft skin, safe physical holding, close to the familiar heartbeat, perhaps the rhythm of a familiar voice that conveys a recognising emotional state long before a word can be understood, the constant body-regulated temperature of milk). Much of this can be replicated with a bottle if the mental state of the parent and baby enables these features. As I outlined in Chapter 3, the baby's experience of the psyche-soma is an intersubjective one. Ogden's concept of the autistic–contiguous mode of organising experience emphasised this early embodied intersubjectivity as basic to ontological security and the floor on which later self experience stands. The mother's internal world is a central part of this psyche-soma.

I have argued that there are psychic reasons for the father, or any 'not mother' object involved in caring at this early stage, to be experienced as different. If we are talking about a man here, this gains significance through the experience of difference at the somatic level. Held against his chest, the baby is cushioned in a different way, receives the pulse of a different heartbeat, hears a different register of voice. When the baby puts her fist up to his face, she feels the bristly quality of his skin, in contrast to the mother's. There are also bodily similarities between the parents: the size and encompassing quality of both parents and probably the firm and secure quality of their holding in comparison to, say, a sibling who tries to cradle the infant in thin arms. This serves as a reminder that generational difference is an ever-present axis that unites adults and differentiates them from the children. Before symbolic thought, which comes later, these are direct sensory experiences ('apperceptions') of difference. Some babies, for example, only settle when picked up by women and, when they are mobile, keep out of reach of any men. They don't have a label of sexual difference at this point, but retrospectively, when sexual and gender differences do impinge on the child's experience, requiring that they be understood and applied to the self, these early sensations acquire their gendered significance, each through a unique life history. According to psychoanalytic theory, at every point meanings work on and reuse prior experience like a crochet hook gathers earlier stitches through its thread in order to create the new stitch. Meanings are not just made up of what is available in current experience.

What this means is that the experience of care from the father or mother (or a surrogate carer, man or woman) is never going to be identical. It is different from the start, for reasons that are given by biological sexual difference. These unsym-bolised early experiences of difference contribute to the later meanings of gender difference too (not least in sexual desire). This does not mean, however, that biology defines appropriate gendered caring roles. My view of the role of biology is not deterministic because sexual differences get caught up in the creative imaginings of the inner world and are used in unique ways to inform a child's struggle with developing a gendered subjectivity. Whereas for Freud gender was reduced to sexual difference (either you had a penis or you did not), in this view, a range of anatomical differences, discovered at different points in life in a wide variety of unpredictable circumstances, will provide the material for fantasy that, in tandem with information from the external world, will subsequently be re-worked. For my purposes here I am interested in *how* it is re-worked; for example, how experience of a father as primary carer signifies in the light of the child's struggle with the knowledge that they have to be either a boy or a girl.

What happens to these 'unthought known' figures of mother and father as the infant develops the capacity to apprehend whole persons, rather than just respond to bundles of more or less familiar sensations? Most psychoanalysts accept that the fantasy of maternal omnipotence (see Chapter 4) contributes to the child's turn to the father as a means of separating from the 'omnipotent' mother, accompanied by a transfer of power to him. Both boys and girls do this, but the boy does it from the position of never being able to 'be' this figure himself, whereas the girl knows she can one day be mother. Juliet Mitchell reminds us, however, that this does not solve the girl's problem immediately:

> [A]ll children want to have babies and both genders have to give this up in the present of their childhood. If they give it up, girls and boys do so differently. Girls know that if they do give up the idea of having babies now, they will be able to have them, and so be in the position of the mother, in future. Boys must give up such thoughts absolutely.
>
> (J. Mitchell 2000: 154)

Classically, boys are seen as identifying with the father and 'disidentifying' with the mother, repudiating what she stands for, not least through failure to come to terms with a difference that leaves them bereft of the creative act of bearing children. Benjamin adds to this picture further by pointing out that the problem 'is not simply that male children disidentify with and then repudiate the mother. It is also that this repudiation involves the psyche in those projective processes . . . that intensify the fear of the other's omnipotence as well as the need to retaliate by asserting one's own omnipotence' (1995: 86). Here we see a further consequence of repudiation. It does not just leave the boy bereft of important parts of his mother, which, through identification, he could have acquired for himself, such as the capacity to care. That is the schizoid part. The paranoid part – the fact that the intolerable parts he has projected are experienced as belonging to the female other – means that he is left with irrational fear of the other/mother. This paranoid–schizoid functioning may end up predominating in a man's relationship to women and children. If so, the prognosis for his capacities to care for a dependent child would be worrying. He would be caught up in the kind of identification with the infant that would preclude the idea that its dependence on its mother could be tolerable. He would denigrate the mother and he would split off caring and project it out, along with other unacceptable parts of the maternal, in such a way that he would be depleted of these parts himself and hate them in the mother, his partner. The negative effects would be two-fold; both on his relationship to the child directly, and indirectly via the child's experience of him in the parental relationship.

Identificatory love

More usually, the depressive position dominates and in this case children have increasingly secure access in their internal worlds to a differentiated figure of the mother who incorporates good and bad parts and who, like the child, can sometimes need care. Elsa First (1988) has observed the leaving games of two-year olds who are working out their feelings about losing their mothers when left at nursery. Benjamin's summary and conclusion is worth quoting at length:

> The children's symbolic play evolved from an aggressive, retaliatory reaction to an identification with the leaving mother who misses the child. In the initial position the child reverses roles and insists that the mother play the child, gleefully ordering her to cry. But soon the glee at reversing the inflicted suffering is mixed with and transformed by identification with the mother's subjective experience of missing the child. . . . In the transition from a retaliatory world of control to a world of mutual understanding, the child gets to recognise that the leaving mother is not only separate but a center of subjective experience not unlike the child's.
>
> (1995: 92–93)

That a child can identify with the mother's experience is a precondition for a capacity to care about her. More broadly, Benjamin argues for a perspective that holds in tension the maternal figure of intrapsychic life (the omnipotent mother) and the mother as subject in her own right that, as First demonstrated, is a figure that is accessible to many two-year-olds, albeit intermittently. This latter figure, moreover, continually confronts the child in the external world, where the real mother comes and goes[6], with many competing demands on her time and attention (see Chapter 4).

The implications for boys of how they come to terms with the loss of their mother are important, as we have seen in Benjamin's distinction between renunciation and repudiation. If dominated by the phantasy of maternal omnipotence, a boy will repudiate all things maternal and deplete himself of those related characteristics such as care. The processes that lead to renunciation are altogether more benign. Benjamin argues that boys' pre-Oedipal identifications with both parents, involving identificatory love, are not obliterated or erased with the traumas associated with

Oedipal threat and loss. If boys come to terms with Oedipal loss more gradually, and in a context where the father does not only represent harsh authority and the threat of (symbolic) castration, but also love, then his coming to terms with the loss associated with being a boy and not like his mother will be bearable and is less likely to result in paranoid–schizoid defences and depletion of the self. The boy can benefit doubly here. First, he can preserve his earlier identificatory love with the mother, so these identifications need not be 'disidentified' with in the name of gender. Second, he can preserve identificatory love with the pre-Oedipal father, even when confronted with the threatening father (in the boy's internal world) of the Oedipal conflict. Again, it is worth keeping in focus the real father (assuming he engaged in the emotional work of care with his infant) who does not in reality change in his capacity to care when the Oedipal child's internal phantasy of him changes:

> To the degree that the characteristics of the other have been lovingly incorporated through identification in the overinclusive phase, loss can be ameliorated by intimacy, and the sequelae of the oedipal phase can be informed more by other-love than by repudiation/idealization.
>
> (Benjamin 1995: 69)

According to Benjamin, girls also turn to the father in identificatory love, an idea that was not acknowledged in Freudian theory, where girls turned to the father in object love; that is, needing to have from him something that they could never have for themselves. Here too it matters whether the father can identify in return.

In the case of a girl's identificatory love with her father, there is a world of difference between a father who returns a daughter's identifications when, say, he is building something in the garden, with 'go and help your mother' and one who finds a spade of a manageable size and shares the job, comfortable with the idea that she can grow up to be like him, despite being a girl. According to Benjamin, it is thus possible 'to integrate the preoedipal identifications of boys with mother and of girls with father as identifications with difference which sufficiently modify the sense of loss, envy and concomitant repudiation' (1995: 102).

What I have set out is an argument that children can use cross-sex identifications to come to terms with loss and work out who they are in relation to the constraints of sexual difference. Cross-gender identifications are different again. Because gender is relatively independent of sex (which is why it is good to preserve both terms rather than conflate them under 'gender' as is now common), the gendered characteristics of the parents need not parallel their sexual difference. Thus it might be that a boy identifies with, for example, the caring relationship that he has experienced more with his father than with his mother, or a girl with the authoritative, rule-observing characteristics of her mother.

Fathers' difference

It may be objected that to hold on to the idea that authority and care (to take the above examples) are gender differentiated and remain so even when identified with in the parent of the other sex is to preserve a traditional notion of gender polarity beyond its historical sell-by date. If enough fathers care for their dependent infants, might these positions be neutralised? My discussion of the unique biological position of the mother and the continuities that emanate from that, suggests that any changes would not be so direct or predictable.

Psychoanalytic thinkers have largely concluded that the structural positions, or functions, represented initially in the child's mind by the two parents (even in their absence, or in non-traditional family forms) continue to be gendered even if the position is taken up by a member of the other sex. This is precisely because of the infant's early experience of the mother's body (or more accurately her 'psyche-soma') as the initial one and the father's – or whoever else represents difference – as the other (see above). Bollas takes the position that 'Rather than emphasise the person of the mother or the father as objects to be internalised, I prefer to speak of them as bearing orders: sets of functions which engage and process the infant.' He goes on to differentiate between these orders and the people who embody them:

> By placing certain attributes under the name of the father (for example interpretation) or mother (for example reverie), I am not saying that the father is incapable of reverie or that the mother is not [sic] without her own form of interpretation . . . It is important to bear in mind that these orders are not descriptions of how all mothers and fathers behave, but of processes associated with and usually conducted by the mother or the father, who assume differing forms of significance for the developing infant.
>
> (1999: 37)

Perhaps this still bears traces of the Freudian position where the paternal order was Oedipal bearer of 'the law', and where he was necessary to force the son out of his dyadic love affair with the mother. This led to the widely adopted position where father is the 'third term' (the object that necessarily follows the first two, baby and mother). Benjamin cites Juliet Mitchell critically for adopting this position, along with other 'Lacanian' feminists. Mitchell concludes that 'To date, the father stands in the position of the third term that must break the asocial dyadic unity of mother and child. We can see that this term will always need to be represented by something or someone' (J. Mitchell 1982: 23, cited in Benjamin 1995: 96). Benjamin disagrees for two reasons (which I do not see as being incompatible with Mitchell's position). First, like many others, she believes that mothers and children are capable of separating without the threat of an Oedipal father. Second, because of her position that the figure of the Oedipal father is not the only experience of the father, that a pre-Oedipal father also exists in the child's mind, she argues that the father can be the 'second second' for the child, which is very different from structurally being the third term: 'what I wish to underscore is the importance of a second adult, not necessarily a male or a father, with whom the child can form a second dyad' (Benjamin 1995: 57). What is important about this figure is 'not yet that he or she loves the mother and seals the triangle, but that he or she creates the second vector, which points outward and on which the triangle can be formed' (ibid).

Characteristically, then, Benjamin is not arguing for either/or but both/and, in this case images of the father emerging in different phases of gender development and coexisting as a tension in the child's experience of the father. Benjamin does not therefore give up the structural difference between mother and father:

> The mother has represented holding, attachment, and caretaking while father has represented the outside world, exploration, freedom. . . . This parental constellation has created a distinct structural position for the rapprochement[7] father, a function that may be played by other figures who represent separate subjectivity. Indeed I would argue that this position is so psychically and culturally important, so distinct from that of the preoedipal father, that it persists despite variation in the role and gender of those who represent it.
>
> (Benjamin 1995: 57)

Benjamin believes that the turn to the father starts with identificatory love. Hence, although it may serve a defensive function to compensate for loss of the mother, 'it is not only defensive, insofar as the ideal father serves symbolically to represent longings that the child may one day hope to realize, as well as the freedom, agency, and contact with the outside world of other people that partially compensate for loss of control' (Benjamin 1995: 58).

The idea of triangular space emphasises the importance of the father, not as a second dyad for the child but as forming a triangle in which the child is placed in a qualitatively different position. This is based on Britton's thinking in which the baby's access to a relationship between two people, both outside itself, gives it a radically new perspective from the one that is inside a dyad. It can experience the quality of that relationship from outside, as witness not participant. The baby can then imagine that there is more than one position to be known from and can imagine his relationship with either of the others being known by the third. In this kind of thinking, the other two positions can be occupied by any other persons. However, if the child does experience being held in mind by the two people who came together to create her or him, it will have a further significance; likewise if he experiences positive qualities in that relationship where he is in the position of the third. All will be important experiences in self development incorporating plural identifications, including those across difference.

Other triangles will each have their own power. I remember an occasion with my mother and my teenage daughter when the subject of my partner came up. My daughter made some deprecating comment about him and my mother's response to her was that when she was a bit older and leaving home, she would be grateful that I had a partner because she would feel free of the responsibility of leaving me on my own. Coming from her grandmother (the woman from whom I, as daughter, had separated), this struck a deep chord in my daughter. I had a strong sensation of her mind working across a new link. In case anyone is falling into the common assumption that this self and gender development, this separation and differentiation, is all over with junior school, this example may act as a reminder that these processes are salient in adolescence and indeed beyond. When people become parents while still not separated from their own parents, the transition from someone who can indulge their own narcissism to someone who must contain not only their own, but also their infant's, frustrations and anxieties is particularly hard.

In this perspective, the categories of 'father' and 'mother' can accommodate others not in that biological position and not necessarily of that sex. There are slippages between the real people, the internal phantasy figures, the 'orders' or functions of the structural position that someone occupies, and so on. None of this means that the originals are identically substitutable. The current growth of interest in people finding their birth parents (even if they have had loving alternative families) demonstrates more than a discourse but also a deep desire to know who your parents are in order to know who you are yourself. The more available two parents are, the more this work will be achieved in the everyday processes of 'going on being'.

Conclusions

My main focus in this chapter has been on fathers' capacity to care and its links with their experiences of becoming boys. More generally, I am asking how the qualities of parents' care will be influenced by their gendered subjectivities and how these have their effects on children's development of their capacities to care as they face the conflicts involved in recognising that they cannot be both sexes. There are some biologically determined losses involved, notably boys' inability to bear and suckle children, but because of the gender system that is based on biological difference, the losses and attendant conflicts are much greater than biological sex on its own would require. I have focused on understanding the mutual identifications within these sexed, gendered and generational relations, in particular thinking about what opens up (and also therefore what closes down) the possibilities of cross-sex and cross-gender identifications. In my psycho-social analysis, I have tried to maintain in tension the use of intra-psychic and real relations approaches. The former helps to avoid a sociological reductionism; the latter, an intrapsychic one. The political conclusion of a sociological view, namely that social changes in gender relations will be directly reflected in changed gendered subjectivities is, I believe, voluntaristic and not evident empirically. The political implications of the kind of psychoanalysis that focused on the archetypal gendered figures of internal phantasy are, on the other hand, pessimistic because there is at best an under emphasis on the effects (albeit mediated) of external reality, in this case how the reality of changes in the gender of parenting, has any effects on subjectivity. By holding together both of these analytical perspectives, I have produced not clear conclusions but – I hope – a sense of just how complex and open-ended are the processes that produce, reproduce and change the gender of care.

In the introduction to this chapter, I asked what features of their own growing up as boys will be likely to affect fathers' capacity to care. This central question was complicated by many other family influences, each with its own real and phantasy dimensions and each experienced differently depending on the developmental phase and the current conflicts being precipitated around separation, difference and loss: the boy's relationship to his father and his father's recognition of his identificatory love; the boy's relationship to his parents' relationship; the arrival of siblings and how this impinges on his position in the family. Broadly speaking, my answer to this question is that much depends on whether, as boys, these fathers succeeded in retaining their positive identifications with maternal capacities to care for them, while at the same time coming to terms with being boys.

6

DIFFERENCE, ETHICS AND THE CAPACITY TO CARE

Ethical life begins the moment we encounter others who are not reducible to
ourselves, and realise that we must negotiate living in the world with them.
(*Soundings* editorial 2004: 16, paraphrasing Arendt)

The simple recognition of a similarity with some other external object that is
recognized as having its own separate existence is a sophisticated achievement.
(Hinshelwood 1991: 319)

Does difference have to mean othering?

The epigraphs above pose, from very different theoretical perspectives, the question
of how human beings experience and respond to similarity and difference between
them and other people. This is recognised as being fundamental to the question
of ethics, as in Levinas' founding of philosophy on an intersubjective ethics of
responding to the Other. Morality resides in the capacity to treat others ethically.
Here the capacity to care meets ethics.

The question of treatment of others has become bound up with the question of
treatment of difference; a conflation that I shall try to undo. It results, as in recent
cultural and feminist theory, from an exclusive emphasis on difference at the
expense of also recognising universal shared characteristics. It has tended to see
difference as insurmountable, particularly in the context of social differences where
direct knowledge is replaced by generalised discourses. This theory has emphasised
the 'othering' that takes place in which difference is imbued with derogatory
meanings. Empirically the othering of difference is a serious and widespread
phenomenon, but that does not make it a universal response.

Likewise, people's responses to the suffering of others vary markedly, even when
they have access to the same discourses, resources and practices. I have explained
this phenomenon developmentally through Kleinian and post-Kleinian object
relations theory which emphasises the relationality of mind. Initially, care depends
on whether a person can think about what is happening that may require care; this
equates with Tronto's dimension of attentiveness. I have used Bion's theory of

100

thinking to understand attentiveness better, especially in its emotional dimension; a theory based on the question how painful or otherwise it is to think this thing. The capacity to care is undermined by splitting as a defence against anxiety. For Klein, individual differences in the ability to hold in mind a bad object are explained by access to depressive functioning. It is paranoid–schizoid functioning, not human nature in general, that leads to the kind of othering that dehumanises the other and exonerates the self from care (for example 'they're not like us so they don't suffer like we would when this kind of disaster hits them'). When such positions become entrenched in dominant discourses, it becomes harder for individuals to access alternative positions, irrespective of their mode of organising experience.

Empirically, it is clear that conflicts, from genocidal to marital, revolve to some extent around difference. In this book so far, my focus has been on relations of care amongst family intimates and I have justified this through the argument that it is in the earliest caring relationships, often parental and especially maternal, that caring subjectivity is forged. I have also argued that it is possible that transformations into caring subjectivity can generalise from maternal care to apply to others in a wider network. Nonetheless, all of my examples so far have been based on face-to-face relations, have assumed embodied meeting of those involved in relationships of care. Does care extend beyond this relatively narrow domain? Do the processes of identification that are fundamental to care extend across distance and difference? If so, how do they work? These questions are highly salient for politics in an institutionalised and globalised world.

I start by considering Levinas' ethical philosophy, hailed recently as making an important contribution to these questions. Levinas' ethics, consistent with his philosophical discourse and the scope of his project, is about universal principles concerning the 'inter-human order', rather than the micro-processes of ethical relating. Nonetheless, there are striking points of contact through the idea of intersubjectivity that serve as bridges between these approaches. With ethics and justice in view, I test out the radically intersubjective model of the self that I have developed in this book in a variety of non-family settings. These, from micro to macro, cover friendship, institutional care, caring across social difference and caring across distance.

Ethics, self and relationship

Ethics is another way of talking about the capacity to care; one that belongs more to the public than the private sphere, more to care for strangers than intimates, more to citizenship than mothering, more to philosophy than psychology. Basically, though, to care for others and the environment that sustains them is to live an ethical life. Levinas also starts from this basic postulate: 'to perceive that we come after an other whoever he may be – that is ethics' (Levinas 1999: 167).

For Levinas, ethics is the irreducible relation of the subject to the other, emanating from the beginning point of being human since life is already a 'being for the other'. Levinas sets out the argument as follows:

> I have attempted to carry out a phenomenology of sociality, starting out from the face of the other man, reading, before all mimicry, in its facial directness, a defenceless exposure to the mysterious forlornness of death, and hearing, before all verbal expressions from the bottom of that weakness, a voice that commands an order issued [signifié] to me not to remain indifferent to that death, not to let the other die alone, i.e., to answer for the life of the other man (...).
>
> (Levinas 1999: 29)

Levinas defines these unconditional obligations towards others in the most stringent way, by specifying not a reciprocal relationship in which one expects to get something back, but an asymmetrical one: 'going to the other where he is truly other' (Levinas 1999: 88). This responsibility both defines human sociality and serves as the core of morality, an exhortation of the most exigeant kind, being not for familiars but strangers and not conditional on one's interests, but unconditional (Sampson 2003).

The concept of transcendence is central in Levinas' understanding of ethical subjectivity because it is 'a way for the distant to give itself' and as such 'appears to be the marker of a paradox of a relation with what is separate' (Hayat, preface to Levinas 1999: ix). For me, this helpfully poses the questions central to this chapter about caring across distance and difference. Transcendence is born of exteriority and 'cannot consequently be felt otherwise than as a subjectivity in crisis, that finds itself facing up to the other, whom it can neither contain, nor take up, and who nonetheless puts it into question' (ibid: xiv). Ogden's concept of the third offers a way of thinking about the unconscious processes that might be at work in this subjectivity 'in crisis'. In terms familiar to psychoanalysis, this is a subjectivity in dynamic conflict as a result of the recurrent unconscious identification of the subject with another, that creates a third intersubjective space which potentially transforms that subject.

In a sense, my book is about how Levinas' commandment might actually be achieved (or fail to be achieved), approached through the lens of the vicissitudes in becoming a person who, in a continuous array of specific settings is or isn't good enough at caring for particular others (individually and collectively). 'Good enough' implies evaluation of the quality of care in how caring about is expressed in practice, and therefore reflects back on the quality of caring about itself. Asking what, when and how is good-enough care runs the risk of normative judgement, which I have tried to address not by avoiding the question but by situating my answers. Another way of looking at what I do in this book in relation to Levinas' ethics is to say that I bring into focus a cluster of reasons why the vast majority of people fail to live up to his primary commandment. At the same time, I maintain what some would see as an optimistic stance regarding the possibility of not othering others, even the 'stranger' or outgroup member. This is based, first on the idea that depressive functioning can often prevail over paranoid–schizoid functioning, given support from containing relationships and structures. Second, it is supported by my argument (Chapter 4) that families and other intimate groupings need not work against extended care (a view often implied in the juxtaposition of private and public) but provide the crucible within which the necessary capacities are initially experienced and fostered. For example, the 'Greenham women' who left their families to protest against the UK's nuclear weapons programme were eschewing the particular needs of intimates in order to care for a very generalised other: the safety of the world from nuclear war (Roseneil 2000).

Levinas' explanation as to how people come to meet these obligations and responsibilities is in the contention that 'the other is already in me'. Perhaps this is the seed of an explanation? His claim here appears not so different from Riviere's Kleinian-inspired 'we are members one of another' or Money Kyrle's more dynamic 'there is a continual unconscious wandering of other personalities into ourselves . . . a multitude made into one' (quoted in Brown 1966: 146–147). In several respects, Levinas' account of subjectivity is consistent with a psychoanalytic understanding. First, he describes an introjection of the other into the self (a moral introjection), without which the psyche could not come into being: I unavoidably suffer from the other's suffering. The self 'does not volunteer, it is enlisted' (Cohen 2002: 41). Second, subjectivity for Levinas is fundamentally conflictual: 'a person would rather not be troubled by another but there before the other, the self . . . is troubled, a moral self and rises to the occasion and aids the other' (Cohen 2002: 56).

At this extreme, care connotes suffering, a reminder of the close linguistic affinity in Anglo-Saxon languages between care and burden, bed of trouble and suffering (Bowden 1997: 9). Levinas' emphasis on suffering, as opposed to pleasure, reminds me of Klein's description of the difficult challenge of facing frustrating reality, relinquishing omnipotence and making reparation. In Levinas' hands, however, these claims imply that the ethical subject has no recourse to defences against the pain of the suffering other, as if they are inevitably – and statically – in the depressive position. His position is therefore consistent with Klein's understanding that ethics, or moral subjectivity in her view, is a characteristic of the depressive position, but not with the later Kleinian view that there is an inevitable oscillation between the paranoid–schizoid and depressive positions, depending on the threats from the external world and the established ways of dealing with these in the internal world (Bion's symbol ps←→d). Object relations theory recognises the same difficulty as Levinas but emphasises the dynamic quality of that conflict. For Benjamin, this conflict is expressed as a permanent tension between omnipotent wishes to control the other and the ability to respect their differences.

A further point of contact between Levinasian ethics and a psychoanalytic account of care is in Levinas' recognition that we have to protect the other from the self, because the danger of our – unethical – human nature is that we will do violence to the other's otherness 'by imposing our self on another self, so as to make the other like me' (Alford 2002: 41). I discussed this in terms of omnipotence and narcissism in Chapter 1, where I raised the question of how people acquire the capacity for accurate identification in the face of such forces. Levinas' answer to this ethical dilemma was for the ego to remain apart as much as possible, to take refuge in a kind of solitude far removed from the care for others – or perhaps more accurately the obligation to care for others – which, for him, is inevitably tainted by controlling omnipotent desires. Here Levinas is taking the position that I share, namely that an ethical attitude to the other (I would say good-enough care) requires recognition of the other's difference from the self. Levinas' categories are, however, too static to capture the possibility of transcending the binary: either undifferentiated connectedness or isolated separation. He cannot envisage the position referred to by Hinshelwood in the epigraph to this chapter. Object relations psychoanalysis describes the vicissitudes in the achievement of separation or its failure to be achieved.

Levinas' view of the ego retreating into separation bears echoes of the masculine autonomous subject that stands in a binary relationship to the intersubjective subject that he espouses as the basis of his ethics. Or perhaps it just emphasises the conflict between individuality and intersubjectivity, between differentiation and intersubjective connection. For me, object relations approaches offer a solution to this dualism in which our selves are made up of internalised parts of others – multiple, but more or less integrated into a relatively coherent self. The dynamic unconscious, when conceived intersubjectively as object relations theory does, conceptualises how we transform others into parts of ourselves (introjection) and parts of ourselves into others (projection). For Levinas, the other in ourselves appears as an unwelcome, albeit unavoidable parasite, 'standing between me and my ego' (Alford 2002: 29); what Levinas calls 'a malady of identity' (ibid). The Levinasian ego is, in Alford's phrase 'a persecuted hostage to the other' (2002: 1): we behave ethically because we can't help it, and not because there is any pleasure in it, stemming from human communion.

It seems to me that this conclusion is rendered unavoidable because of Levinas' singular vantage point of the ethical subject, represented in his test that care be exercised across the distance separating oneself from the weaker other. His ethical perspective is therefore never widened to include the two-way dynamic flow of intersubjectivity between the giver and receiver of care. As Kristeva comments of Levinas, there is no concept of mingling as communion, no understanding of the joys of fluidity (cited in Alford 2002: 71). Levinas' ethical first principle that the other must be protected from being reduced to the same allows no me in you and you in me. Consequently, Levinas rules out the embrace of pleasures as well as burdens of care. This limitation is exacerbated because, for Levinas, Others are abstract, never particular, and consequently he is unable to consider the effects of their qualities as fellow humans. Alford describes Levinas' paradigm of the self and its relationships here as having only two values – self and other – like an on/off switch. In this view, there is no room for the mutuality of desires that would mean that both care and pleasure could exist in the same act. Alford gives the example of sexual relations (op cit: 55) and argues that, for Levinas, it is as if all sex would be exploitative because, if it pleases one person, the other must be suffering from that selfishness. In practice there is a distinction between exploitative and consensual sex. In the latter, two people are both 'using' the other for their pleasure but in the knowledge that the pleasure is mutual, which enhances and amplifies that of each.

Interestingly, Levinas' assumptions reflect the early ruthlessness of the infant's demand on the mother, demands that she cannot ignore because the infant's life depends on her. If this is Levinas' unconscious model for the ethical relationship, it makes added sense of his emphasis on the Other's precariousness in the face of death as the defining need of the other that demands attention ('not to remain indifferent to that death, not to let the other die alone, i.e., to answer for the life of the other man'; op cit). This is the basic state of the infant when in need of maternal containment; a state described as 'falling for ever' (Winnicott 1974: 104) or 'falling apart' (Bick 1986: 296). Bion describes it as 'nameless dread', the result of the mother's lack of reverie; reverie that the infant needs to make its fear of dying tolerable (Bion 1967: 116):

> . . . that the mother should have treated the infant's cry as more than a demand for her presence. From the infant's point of view, she should have taken into her, and thus experienced, the fear that the child was dying. It was this fear that the child could not contain. [. . .] An understanding mother is able to experience the feeling of dread, that this baby was trying to deal with by projective identification, and yet retain a balanced outlook.
>
> (Bion 1967: 104)

It is originally in the maternal position that this demand is so incontrovertible and so exclusively one way because of the infant's total dependency. It is a demand for containment, and not just for presence. Moreover Levinas, despite echoing this maternal position in his ethical commandment, leaves out the other aspect of maternal subjectivity, its status as a paradigmatic case of intersubjective experience that transcends the individual woman. His reformulation of transcendence as what accompanies the birth of human subjectivity perhaps unconsciously draws on this more literal meaning: the maternal body and maternal subjectivity as foundational in the birth of a new subjectivity.

Levinas explicitly uses the paradigm of motherhood to describe the infinite, burdensome responsibility of care for the other: the maternal psyche was for him the example, par excellence, of the other being in oneself and the basis for ethical life. However, in my view, the strivings of 'human nature' for control of the other, the strivings that are a normal expression of omnipotence in the helpless infant, are mitigated by the kind of developments of self that Klein regarded as inherently moral (see Chapter 3). Klein sees the selfishness of infantile love as modifying itself into a genuine love through the acquisition of concern for the other, and the capacity for reparation. This has sometimes been called 'love's knowledge', the ability to love someone for who they are, without intruding into their otherness, an intrusion led by one's needs to make them suitable to oneself. Love's knowledge is, in my view, a core characteristic of good-quality care, in which caring is guided and motivated by what is best for that other person, and one's own needs are recognised as quite distinct.

According to object relations theory, connectedness, stemming from positive identifications with others, enables concern, sympathy, compassion, and therefore reparation and care. These make up the self and they continue to link us to others. Levinas describes these affects of connectedness as '*transferts de sentiments*' or transferred affects. This too recalls the object relations principle of projection and introjection of affects, relations and parts of objects. However, transferred affects appear in Levinas as a regrettable weakness because they infect the self. This conclusion again derives from Levinas' starting point of an ego or self that needs to protect itself from connection to others because only suffering results. It is like psychoanalysis assuming that all introjections involve bad objects, which would make it blind to the rich and fulsome additions to the personality that are achieved through identifications with others.

Identification and difference

In Levinas' conceptualisation, it is hard to see how the ethical subject can be connected and differentiated at the same time. This is a similar binary as in the work of the early ethics of care theorists (see Chapter 2) and which the second wave has identified as a weakness in its policy and political applications (see Chapter 1). It is therefore a crucial theoretical issue to clarify if my account of the capacity to care is to work and the understanding of identification is central to its clarification. Identification has been theorised within a paradigm of sameness and it has required more recent developments in the psychoanalytic understanding of gender development to develop the idea of identification across difference (Benjamin 1995). Indeed, Benjamin uses the phrase 'identification with difference' as 'an intentionally paradoxical formulation [which] is meant to suggest an identification that crosses the line that demarks what we are supposedly like, the boundary that encloses the identical' (1995: 53).

Identification is a supremely relational phenomenon, often unavailable to consciousness and resistant to conscious intention. It is also a difficult and precarious achievement; one whose vicissitudes account for a lot of the troubles that routinely occur in relations between people and groups. According to Hinshelwood (1991), identification is about relating to another person on the basis of experiencing similarities with one's self. However, it comes in many forms, which vary depending on how successfully one is able to recognise the other as separate from oneself. 'The simple recognition of a similarity with some other external object that is recognized as having its own separate existence is a sophisticated achievement' (Hinshelwood 1991: 319). When identification occurs without recognition of the separate existence of the other, troubles can start that lead to failure to care, even occasionally when it is wrapped up as care. This clarification of the workings of identification as an intersubjective process is vital. Identification does not preclude differentiation, but depends on it for the accuracy and therefore the quality of caring about.

Benjamin has theorised identification through and with difference in detail in respect of the acquisition of gender identity (see Chapter 5). The processes of separation and differentiation are more successfully achieved through renunciation rather than repudiation, because renunciation leaves the attachment relatively unscathed:

> ... disowned identifications [of the boy] with the mother reappear in feelings of loss and envy ... Women's and men's identifications are always multiple and the upshot of relinquishing crucial identifications with difference is that difference is defensively incorporated into rigid representations, rather than recognised in tension with commonality.
>
> (Benjamin 1995: 17)

Difference is never absolute in reality, although it can feel so, supported by polarised discourses linked to a paranoid–schizoid mode of organisation of experience. Difference is always accompanied by similarity; ultimately found in human universals like pain and joy, fear, loss and need.

In practice, the difficulty of what Hinshelwood characterises as a sophisticated achievement is recognised in caring for. In their discussion of nursing, Benner and Wrubel emphasise the difficulty of finding a balance between 'the poles of burdensome emotional identification and that severance from the person in pain that creates a schism in the nurse's own experience. Anything more is self indulgence, anything less, self estrangement' (cited in Bowden 1997: 112). Note that severance does not just estrange the nurse from the patient but from herself. This can be explained in a theory of self where 'we are members, one of another'. This delicate balance raises again the question of the desirability and limits of identification. I want to stress the importance of realistic identification. We need to identify with the ill person's suffering in order to respond appropriately. This does not require that the nurse confuse her own self, who is not in physical pain, with the patient who is. The reality of her separate body tells her that they are different, yet she also feels compassion because she is imaginatively able to identify with the pain, drawing on a whole history of meaning, experience and fantasy. In this way it becomes possible to think of connection and differentiation as different dynamic processes which may be more or less in conflict with each other. A friend told me about her experience of caring for a close relative partially paralysed from an accident. Through the practice of caring she learned in detail what it meant to have no sensations or functions in most of one's body. Yet the baseline experience was of the separateness of their bodies, one healthy and the other only partially functioning. Identification coupled with differentiation, added to particularity and practice, make for the most recognising and accurate care. The individual reality of bodily sensations, distinguished from imagination and fantasy, provide an important aid to such differentiation. Identification with difference depends on accepting or being able to discern reality, another characteristic of the depressive position.

Peta Bowden discusses maternal caring as one example (the other is colonisation) of ethically contentious caring, a debate that emphasises the oppressive power relations involved. She takes issue with the argument that responses developed within oppressive relations of domination and submission are necessarily negative (1997: 18), specifically challenging those feminists who see care in asymmetrical power relations as compromised. For example, in women's friendships with men, Claudia Card suggests, women's care is likely to be a 'survival strategy for women whose institutionalised dependence on men gives us reasons to be responsive to men's interests and values' (cited in Bowden 1997: 90). In this situation, where women are not equal subjects, their concern and attachment, according to Card, may result from their own 'poor self definition and the desire for approval' (ibid). Similarly, Sandra Bartky argues that caring relationships with social superiors can produce a 'tendency to dissolve one's sense of one's own reality' (ibid). They can, but whether they do depends on the characteristics of those involved.[1] In my terms, the danger here is that the social power of the cared for enables him (or her) to indulge his infantile omnipotence; that is, psychically to deny the frustration of the dependent aspects of his reality by using the carer as an extension of his own desires. Social power facilitates this but the reassertion of early omnipotence is not an inevitable consequence of social power, rather it depends on the person's relational life history; notably if there were others who were capable of establishing subject–subject relations. The same goes for the carer; and these come together in the caring relationship.

The different emphases in this debate hinge on the primacy accorded either to the kind of power involved in relations of recognition or power relations given externally as a result of differences in social status, for example, sex and ethnicity. Benjamin's Hegelian account of the power relations of recognition is useful in extending and rendering more psycho-social the analysis of social power differences. Her model concerning the conflict involved in asserting oneself and needing the other was based on Hegel's discussion of the master–slave relationship. If in his omnipotence, the master refuses to recognise the slave, he is at the same time negating the agent who has the power to recognise him as master:

> We might call this the dialectic of control: if I completely control the other, then the other ceases to exist, and if the other completely controls me, then I cease to exist. A condition of our own independent existence is recognising the other. True independence means sustaining the essential tension of these contradictory impulses; that is, both asserting the self and recognising the other. Domination is the consequence of refusing this condition.
>
> (Benjamin 1990: 53)

For power relations theorists, the tension is assumed inevitably to break down, culminating in domination. For Benjamin, in contrast, its ideal 'resolution' lies in its continuation as a constant tension presenting the possibility of 'true independence'. Power relations cannot be automatically read off social differences: when the effects of social power differences are clearly oppressive, these are nevertheless complicated by the power dynamics of dependency, care and the need for recognition.[2]

On the continuum of differentiation, people vary (from each other as well as in different situations) in how realistically they are differentiated. On one end is narcissistic omnipotence leading to the attempt to control the one whose otherness is denied. On the other end is effective differentiation: 'I am not you. Your pain and pleasure are not mine.' The other process is identification. At one end of this continuum, I feel your pleasure and pain through identification. At the other end, I disidentify. In this case, through splitting and projection, you become the other. You represent things I cannot tolerate, in myself and therefore in you also. It seems that Levinas conflates these two processes of differentiation and identification (as I argued in Chapter 1 that Tronto did through her use of the term 'overidentifica- tion'). His conflation is perhaps occasioned by his usage of the binary Other–Same, as opposed to other–self.[3] This leads to a pessimistic logic whereby difference is equated with otherness. If the two axes are separated, if indeed they are theorised as being potentially independent of each other (imagine two orthogonal axes on a graph), otherness would not necessarily follow from difference. In other words, one can in principle care about others (and potentially be cared about as well) whether or not the other is different. This is not possible in the paranoid–schizoid position, however; it relies on the achievements of ambivalence and tolerance of reality characteristic of the depressive position.

Levinas shares a further suggestive similarity with psychoanalysis: his interest in the move from a two-person scenario to the arrival of a third party, which provides 'the proximity of a human plurality' (1999: 101). At this point, one is forced to ask 'which one, in that plurality, is the other par excellence?' (op cit: 102). This for Levinas is 'the question of justice' (ibid). In relations of justice, unlike relations of charity, 'the other has no privilege with respect to me' (ibid) and rights enter the equation, as Levinas explains in response to a question about his 'attempt to return to justice from what one might call charity' (1999: 175). Charity (also called mercy) he equates with the 'unlimited obligation toward the other', but 'before the multiplicity of human beings [this] becomes justice [which nonetheless] should flow from, issue from, the pre-eminence of the other' (op cit: 175–176).

Individuality, individualisation and friendship

A child's discovery of its mother as a subject in her own right is not straightforward or clear cut. First there is the young baby's discovery that its mother is not an extension of its omnipotent desires. This in itself is long-winded, as it consists of different moments; for example, with the advent of a new distinction that at a toddler age 'Separation consists not so much of losing mother's presence but losing control of her coming and going' (Benjamin 1994: 134). Within different social arrangements from those that pertain in the contemporary West, this is going to happen very differently, for example in the case of extended childcare responsibilities. It will also be affected by cultural practices, which may ritualise separation at a certain age, particularly in the case of boys. Within nuclear families, an older baby also experiences its mother in the triangular relationship with the father or mother's partner or other siblings.[4] Here it can experience her via another's point of view and discover, for example, if she has the right to make choices for herself. In cultures where family males have decisive authority over women, the girl and boy will soon learn, with different results, how she is positioned. A recent study of witchcraft in contemporary Northern Ghana suggests that it is when women appear to be subjects in their own right that they are punished as witches (Badoe 2005). In this way patriarchal gender relations are reproduced. Children's experience of the mother will therefore also depend on women's freedoms. In the nineteenth century, women in Europe still had precious little opportunity to shape their own lives; the twentieth century has been a story of what Beck and Beck-Gernsheim (1983/2002: 55) call the 'many little steps in education work and family' which combined to create an intensifying rate of change in which women could move 'away from "living for others" towards "a bit of a life of our own"' (ibid). Beck and Beck-Gernsheim believed that women's transition from this position (exemplified for them in 1980s Germany) demonstrated a trend towards individualisation.

What light can object relations theory's emphasis on the struggles involved in separation and the lifelong conflicts involved in differentiation cast on the claims of individualisation theory? Individualisation refers to a historical tendency that affects not only the regimes in which selves develop but, in an indirect way, the formation of those selves across the lifespan and across generations. This tendency is likely to emphasise the separate, self-governing potential of human beings. In European settings, this process started with the modern period and was both expressed and influenced by thinkers such as Descartes and Kant, both notorious for claiming the separate, unitary, rational character of individuals. However, actual subjectivities are recalcitrant and not the direct effects of dominant discourses or even the combination of practices, relations, discourses and circumstances that make up the social and material environment. Historical tendencies, such as that towards individualisation, will draw out and render thinkable certain human potentials but other tendencies do not disappear. Intersubjectivity of the kind that I have tried to render thinkable in this book does not disappear. It continues to exist, often as the unthought known, to appear in desires, practices and relations however structured (love and loss, sex and care, for example).

Being able to shape one's life through one's own choices is seen as almost definitional of individualisation. What happens in cases where people are maximally free from the constraints characteristic of traditional living arrangements? Roseneil (2007 forthcoming) examines the claims of individualisation theory to ask what effects on care have been produced by the weakening of family structures and of the sexual and gender arrangements that have characterised them. Intimate and personal life increasingly takes place outside the family and it is within networks of friends that support, care and love is sought in its place: 'friendship is of foundational and particular importance in the lives of lesbians and gay men' (Roseneil 2004: 411). These, and non-cohabiting heterosexuals, she argues, are the people who are most 'individualised', but rather than seeing them as individual and solitary, as individualisation theorists such as Bauman and Sennett do, she emphasises the alternative expressions of relationality that characterise friendship networks. In other words, individualisation, despite its discursive emphasis on self sufficiency, does not involve relinquishing relationality but creates different channels and structures for it.

Friendship has been seen as a paradigm case of symmetrical, egalitarian, reciprocal and intimate care in relationships; a contrast to the idea of care as a self-sacrifice and burden. Aristotle's concept of '*philia*' captures this idea and offers a useful contrast to the care model based in the mother–child relationship. Friendship, unlike family 'ties', is a relationship of choice and therefore a step removed, on a continuum of social distance, from the foundational character of family relation-ships: 'friendship is a significantly different relationship from that of mothering, lacking controlling institutions and firm cultural expectations and conventions' (Roseneil 2004: 414). This is not to say that friendship is of a different, rationally chosen character altogether, however. The contemporary psychoanalytic emphasis on lateral family relationships (see Chapter 3) stresses the importance of early sibling relationships in self formation and how these dynamics (of love and hate, sameness and difference) will inform later lateral relationships. It is probably significant that Aristotle's and Foucault's models of *philia* were based on friend-ships between men, where the original maternal relationship is, transferentially speaking, most distant. *Philia* refers to an 'attachment based on mutual concern of each person for the other for his own sake (Bowden 1997: 65), when, according to Aristotle (1940), 'each has been found loveable and been trusted by the other' (Nichomachean Ethics 1156: 628–629). This model of relationship is therefore implicitly based on the assumption that successful differentiation can coexist with identification to produce accurate recognition and enable friends to be subjects in their own right:

> Friendship is for those . . . whose comfort is sufficient for them to want merely to share rather than to lose their identity. And they enter into friendship as an act of radical choice. Friendship, in this sense is the performance art of freedom.
>
> (Sullivan 1998: 212, cited in Roseneil 2004: 414)

Sullivan's position here seems to be rather voluntaristic. Can care among friends be given and received from a position of equality? The empirical study of friendship offers the possibility of seeing if care can be transacted by equals who can, in my terms, identify with the other from a position of differentiation. I extend this as the ideal of 'maternal development' (see Chapter 4), which gradually succeeds the necessarily asymmetrical care relationship between mother and infant. It is an empirical question how care in friendship relationships works in practice (Roseneil

2007 forthcoming) and if and how it diverges from the care forged in family relationships.

Nonetheless, my theoretical starting point would draw on the developmental insights that inform this book. The infant's early subjectivity, forged in its dependency with the mother is never obliterated. It is modified, not least by sibling and equivalent peer relationships, but continues to exist in the recesses of the unthought known, energised by desire and anxiety. It is expressed in the transference relationship of everyday life, particularly where care is concerned, because of the dependency it evokes. On the other hand, friends may be freer of these transferences than, for example, sexual partners. Roseneil (2004: 413) quotes a twenty-eight-year-old heterosexual woman who participated in her research as 'speaking for many' when she said 'I think a friendship is for life, but I don't think a partner is . . . I'd marry my friends. They'd last longer.' (The paradox is that if people did so, the relationship would probably be threatened by the desires and investments that are more pronounced, if not qualitatively different, in sexual relationships.) Whereas equality in friendship relationships is an ideal, to the extent that lateral relationships derive transferentially from sibling relationships, the power struggles involved there, of sameness and difference, also involve what Juliet Mitchell calls the 'law of the mother' (Chapter 3) and would not be immune to the traces of vertical relationships permeating lateral ones. Likewise, to some extent transferences from sibling relationships will anyway affect all care relationships, not just those at the cutting edge of social change. A further consideration is that friendship dynamics are often created not in dyadic relationships but in group constellations, often based on members of similar age, like siblings.

Blum (1987) uses the example of friendship to explore the importance of particularity in the care and ethics that characterise friendship. According to Bowden, his work 'highlights the moral significance of personalized affection, concern and compassion in fostering the good of other persons for their own sake' (1997: 77). Particularity, the key ethical feature of the care that characterises friendship, refers to the uniqueness of each specific relationship and its existence over time: 'the quality of our responses, the responsibility we take on, our loyalty and concern, are all grounded in this particularity'; namely 'their specific needs, beliefs, aspirations, behaviour and the whole way of being that makes them who they are' (Blum 1987, cited in Bowden 1997: 79). Each friendship is different and, in moulding our care to each, we also demonstrate our capacities to recognise their difference from ourselves. Levinas focuses on absolute difference, captured in his concept of alterity. In the specifics of ethical relations, however, I would see the experience of absolute difference as a result of splitting and projection and contrast it with the possibility of experiencing a kaleidoscopic mixture of every gradation of similarity and difference possible on every facet of each other's subjectivity. In Blum's description, we return to the principle of being able to recognise difference in the other; being able to recognise the other in her own right. It also emphasises the way this happens over time and with increasing knowledge of the other.

Aristotle's *philia* also assumes that the adult parties in a friendship are capable of self care as well as care, which is another reason why this model of care can be understood as free of the burden of dependent care. Levinas' tragic view of ethics shares in the deep-rooted Judaeo-Christian assumption that the obligation to care for others is in conflict with selfish desires. There is some truth in this, presumably reflecting the dominance of the mother–child paradigm, which ideologically, if not in practice, is represented as 'selfless'. The self worth and self care involved in friendship offers 'a healthy alternative to the complete self-effacement sometimes portrayed as "good mothering" in the popular press' (Groenhout 1998: 181, cited in Roseneil 2004: 415). In contrast, Greek thought regarded care for others and self care as expressions of the same ethics (Rabinow 2000), rather than in opposition, as came to be the case during the Christian period.

According to Michel Foucault, the Ancient Greeks believed that self care and care for others were part and parcel of the same ethic; that care of the self was ethical in its own right (Rabinow 2000: 287). Later, during the spread of Christianity, the idea that 'care of the self thoroughly permeated moral reflection' became suspect and in time 'being concerned with oneself was readily denounced as a form of self love, a form of selfishness or self interest in contradiction with the interest to be shown in others or the self sacrifice required' (ibid). I want to re-assert for contemporary ethics what Foucault took to be the postulate of Ancient Greek morality; namely 'that a person who took proper care of himself would, by the same token, be able to conduct himself properly in relation to others and for others' (ibid).

The derivation of this principle from an epoch and a culture very different from late modern individualisation is reassuring. It supports the current search for a way of understanding care relations that is consistent with individuality and can transcend the individualism of late modern culture. Of course Aristotle's ideal of friendship depended on the gendered splitting of men's and women's autonomy and care. Privileged men in Ancient Greece did not have to struggle to be subjects in their own right in the way that women, and in a particular way mothers, did and do today. The conditions for this individuality, this particular form of self expression are, as I have shown, rooted in the intersubjective development of the differentiated self in early care relationships. These are therefore also implicated in the development of self care, connected to how feelings of self worth are acquired, as Turp argued (see Chapter 3).

Institutional care

For Blum, as we saw, an act of friendship derives its meaning through the particularity of the concern and care of that person for the friend, rather than 'an expression of general responsiveness'. This has been debated in relation to nursing care, where the particularity of care is increasingly under threat from the imposition of large-scale administrative systems that depersonalise nursing care. Under systems of administrative care, it is not just the person being cared for but the nurse or other professional health-care worker who suffers loss of meaning and satisfaction from the absence of particularity in the care relationship (Benner and Wrubel 1989). In these ways we cannot, as Blum points out, reduce care to calculations of interests of those involved.

The ideas of caring as citizenship and citizenship as requiring care (Sevenhuijsen 1998) have been limited by the split of public and private discourses and the relegation of caring to the private sphere, whereas citizen roles are in the public sphere. However, there is also a reality-based criterion for differentiating care for intimates (private sphere) and public care; namely our access to the particularities of those others about whom we are expected (and expect ourselves) to care. According to Bowden, the feeling of concern for the other and theirs for oneself is part of the 'affective dimension of nurturance' (1997: 165), which is antithetical to the 'impersonal, generalizing and quantifying processes' of institutional forms of care. These can overwhelm particularistic attentiveness and transform it into administrative care.

The idea of particularity can also usefully be refined with a psycho-social perspective. Although it refers to such realities of relationship as the detailed knowledge that is gathered over time, this reality is mediated to a greater or lesser extent by defences against anxiety. Menzies' ground-breaking study of why trainee nurses were being lost to the profession in critical numbers (1960) showed that the profound anxieties produced by working with patients' pain, suffering and death were unconsciously defended against through the social systems of hospital wards: the rigid rules and routines, the constant change of wards, the concentration on technical practices and the objectification of patients. This enabled medical staff to keep a safer distance from the pain of others. However, it also detracted from the human contact and wish to care that often motivated trainees, who left in droves. Clearly, defensive distancing affects cultural and institutional practices as well as relationships in the private sphere.

In what follows, I take an example of institutional change led by one particular researcher and campaigner James Robertson and his wife Joyce. My purpose is to argue for the importance of identification in this process and show how accurate enough identification across social difference is not only possible but an important aspect of ethical conduct in the public realm.

I introduce a further important theoretical element here, namely what effect available language and discourse has on caring relationships and moral subjectivity. In Chapter 1, I outlined positioning theory and used the example of Skeggs' analysis of the effect of gendered and classed positions on care. Positioning theory maintains that the dominance of discourses is highly influential, if not determining, in the meanings that are available about care, which thus affect caring behaviour. In this short case study, I modify this perspective by considering combined psychological and social influences.

In the post-war British context, James Robertson and his wife Joyce pursued a successful campaign to enable parents to have more contact with their hospitalised children and to change the nursing regime in children's wards. The pre-war treatment of children in British hospitals was an expression of a regime of power in which the child was construed through a medicalised discourse that was blind to the suffering experienced, particularly by young children, when they were separated from their families and familiar environments to be treated in hospital. James Robertson was a purveyor of a new discourse, the attachment discourse. He was conducting the field work for John Bowlby on a project 'to observe and describe the behaviour of young children during and after separation from the mother' (Robertson and Robertson 1989: 10).

Where doctors and nurses typically construed a happy ward as a quiet one where children had 'settled' after a period of temporary upset after admission, Robertson saw evidence of the phases through which children were said to move, following an attachment discourse, in response to separation from an attachment figure: 'those who had been in hospital for some months had moved from Protest and Despair into the third phase which I called Denial/Detachment (denying the wish for relationships)' (Robertson and Robertson 1989: 15). The mental health consequences of a long period in this phase for long-stay especially very young children were serious, in Robertson's view. He sought and found evidence of this through long-term follow up of children who returned home after hospitalisation.

As well as going into children's wards with a different discourse, Robertson was able to identify with the children he met there, despite the distress this caused him. He used an emotional mode of knowing that chimed with the theoretical discourse of attachment and loss he had espoused. He achieved this despite being an adult, a man and someone who had his attachments and health intact. (He was also probably of a different class to many of the children that he observed.) Evidently, these dimensions of social and power difference did not function in a determinist way to 'other' the children that he met. His identification also influenced his choice of method. He filmed children over time in hospital because it came closest to what he called the 'actuality'. In its proximity to the children's emotions it facilitated channels of identification that were crucial in enabling viewers to see distress where before they had seen trouble, a necessary precedent to changes in practice. In Robertson's words: 'when told by the visual medium the story was powerful; it [the film *John*] pierced defences and caused much disturbance in viewers. The reactions of a few colleagues convinced us we had a bomb on our hands' (op cit: 89). The campaign extended an ethic based on care to one based on justice, as the Robertson's engaged institutionally and politically to change systems that would provide just treatment for hospitalised children.

This line of argument implies that Robertson was capable of identifying with the children where the doctors and nurses were not and this is suggested by the evidence but raises the question why. A psycho-social, as opposed to a psychological, explanation, includes the idea of the discourses and practices along which identification can be channelled to facilitate it. From a constructionist position, we can say that this new knowledge, inserted into a nexus of power–knowledge–practice relations, produced a new truth of the child subject, psychological rather than physical; an emotional, relational one, emphasising a child suffering a loss of attachment. This is convincing as far as it goes. It is probable that without the emergence of this new discourse, Robertson would not have seen what he did see in the behaviour of young hospitalised children. A discourse determinist answer is that medical staff saw through the lens of a discourse of the individual 'settled' child. This can be refined by pointing to the institutional practices that supported the discourse, for example a system of job allocation that meant that nurses were not allocated to particular children. Robertson identifies both discursive and institutional factors but he goes further and provides what I call a psycho-social explanation:

> They [doctors and nurses] had inherited a system of care that was geared to ensuring that the system functioned smoothly with the focus of attention on physical illness, and were defended against recognising the distress and danger for mental health caused. . . . The fact that under-fives cried on being visited was noted as 'trouble', not as a danger sign.
>
> (op cit: 8)

What Robertson adds to a social explanation is the idea of doctors' and nurses' defences against distress and trouble. In other words, the pre-war nexus of power–knowledge–practice in children's hospital wards was not only socially, but psychologically mediated.

Sevenhuijsen comments that, without rights, care can be reduced to charity (1998: 144). She challenges the dichotomy of care and justice, which, she says, is 'at its sharpest when justice is framed in the epistemological paradigm of distributive justice in which abstract rationality, impartiality and sameness are paramount' (1988: 145). Justice can be reframed in terms of social practices: social justice, which 'can encompass measures of what constitutes fair and reasonable treatment' (ibid). The Robertsons' campaign is such an example: a campaign for fair and reasonable treatment of hospitalised children, a 'unit of concern' (Pogge 2002: 169) that deals in multiples defying face-to-face relations and risks being robbed of specificity and therefore stripped of emotional experience.[5] That it was based on an ethic of care, dependent on James Robertson's capacity to care across difference and therefore to challenge an uncaring institutional regime, illustrates how the dichotomy of care and justice ethics can be transcended. His capacity, according to my theoretical account, had a basis in his openness to identification with difference. Although this began with particular individual children, it was generalised without becoming abstract so as to be applicable to institutions and regimes that he never personally encountered. Such justice principles depend on thinking of the +K kind (see Chapter 2). Emotionally informed imagination permits care to transcend the face-to-face, powered by identifications that can generalise from individuals to groups. Of course, it is useful that these are abstracted into general principles ('Love thy neighbour as thyself') but only if the principle can be re-experienced in a real or imagined setting that puts it back in touch with the identificatory affect that gives it life.

Distance, othering and care

This is precisely the thread that Dobson (2006: 182) draws out of his critique of 'thin' cosmopolitanism within political theory and international relations discourses: 'Cosmopolitanism needs to bring distant strangers near to us in a way that references to common humanity appear not to do.' He discusses nearness, not only in spatial terms but in terms that suggest psychological and relational nearness ('nearness to vulnerable, suffering and disadvantaged others', op cit: 171) but asks how we can turn strangers into friends and 'neighbours'. My discussion addresses this question in two ways. First, I have discussed the ways that people's plight can be brought near by the representation of specific cases, as in my illustration of Robertson's film, which provided access to what Blum would call particularity. Second, using the psychoanalytic theory of identification, I have inferred the psycho-social processes that would explain how concern and care are possible at a distance and, on the other hand, how difference and distance can be turned into the defensive distance of othering in the paranoid–schizoid mode of organising experience. How do these principles apply when we consider examples of care across long distances?

In the face of consistent and ongoing exploitation of people in the developing countries by those in the developed ('how can severe poverty of half of humankind continue?'; Pogge 2002: 3, cited in Dobson 2006: 165), it is important to pose the question of how far capacities of identification can extend across social distance and difference, and under what cultural, political, discursive and psychological conditions. The psychological question is not separate from the others, but is part of a psycho-social one, because identifications are enabled and disenabled by discourses and cultural practices, such as charitable giving.

I started considering this just after an earthquake under the Indian Ocean had precipitated the largest-scale disaster ever recorded. The tsunami disaster also precipitated the biggest ever charitable response across distance and difference, from Western individuals, groups and governments. How can this be explained? When it comes to action, those who are at a distance must rely on administrative care; money donated to huge organisations, which is turned into shipments of goods whose type and appropriateness is decided by experts, sent to a place whose name we will not know, used in ways whose particulars I find difficult to imagine. This evidently did not put people off: perhaps it encouraged them?

Titmuss (1970) argued that the British system of gift of blood, rather than payment for it, was used by donors as a rare opportunity to contribute to the general good, anonymously and voluntarily. Nonetheless, recent advertising to encourage blood donation uses the image of giving to a specific individual, presumably because market research has found this to be effective. These two channels of motivation need not be mutually exclusive. Indeed, they combine in a way that protects donors from the discomfort of face-to-face giving (Ignatieff 1984), in which the giver is confronted physically with the asymmetry of need in the relationship and the consequent guilty discomfort.

In circumstances such as the tsunami disaster, identifications with human suffering are bolstered by discourses and practices of charity that facilitate action and help retain a balance between being overwhelmed by the horror of the disaster and holding it at such a distance that it is banished from the mind and therefore from the possibility of action. The perspective of realistic differentiation suggests that, despite geographical distance and cultural difference, identification has been possible by westerners via universals such as suffering from the loss of family and the basic security of a home. At the same time, differentiation remains realistic: 'I did not suffer'. This provides a certain kind of emotional distance while permitting the carer to hold in mind (be attentive to) the suffering of others.

Charitable giving is an example of care across physical and cultural distance and difference, enabled by identifications with human suffering. In a shop I visited the following day, the shopkeeper raised the subject of the tsunami disaster and said she could not get it out of her thoughts. What was the concrete content of those thoughts she was having, at such a distance from the lives of those involved? My identifications were channelled by particular images and stories culled from the media and I recognised the skill of journalists to represent the tragedies of hundreds of thousands through selected stories, usually of family members: the orphaned child, the bereft mother, the tearful and despairing father, who were given names, faces and locations. Stories and images concerning the loss of parents and children had a particularly strong impact on me; presumably via a double identification as both parent and child. This is a globalised, media facilitated version of Blum's principle of particularity which provides channels in which identifications can flow. The shopkeeper gave the example of Richard Attenborough's daughter and grand-daughter, who died in the tsunami. Perhaps the man's celebrity status and British identity provided more particular channels for her identifications, brought it 'closer to home', with the dangers of parochialism that this suggests.

As Gillian Rose points out in her exploration of the geographies of proximity and distance, globalisation makes many insistent demands for care: from welcoming asylum seekers to boycotting the products of sweatshops in the developing world (2006). The use of textual representations has historically been powerful in achieving identificatory proximity, for example in the anti-slavery campaigns to get white Europeans to care about the cause of black slaves. From the 1860s, photography was also used and is now ubiquitous in representing the lives of people in distant places, including in the way demands for care are made. Some visual images have been hugely influential (Monk 1989) but many are routinely binned; for example, a haunting image of a tortured person on the front of a leaflet on behalf of Amnesty International (Rose 2006). Edwards talks about the 'rawness' of a visual image (2001) as part of its emotional power, and Cohen asks how come those who see visual evidence of such suffering can exist in states of denial (2001).

Conclusions

In this chapter, I have attempted to provide an account of how ethical obligations are experienced and achieved, to complement the abstract nature of Levinas' commandment of unconditional responsibility for the Other. My account can be summed up in the idea of 'love's knowledge'. I have argued that, developmentally speaking, our capacity to care derives from the qualities of our primary relationships and also explored the significance of the particularistic nature of caring about. 'Caring about' flourishes or is compromised in different ways as a result of early primary relationships and the way these extend across the lifespan and across various forms of group, community, institution and network, supported or undermined by practices and discourses that have implications for care. The reform in children's hospital wards in 1950s London provided an example of the power of institutional policy, practice and dominant discourses to blindfold compassionate identification. It also showed how, with the help of a new discourse and through the capacity to identify with difference, individuals can exercise caring agency that transcends those constraints. Robertson's campaign not only enabled others to identify through the use of a visual medium of representation and the particularity of an individual case but he extended an ethic of care into a campaign for justice by generalising and extracting general principles on which changed rights could be based.

7

CONCLUSIONS

At the beginning of Chapter 1, I posed five sets of questions about the capacity to care that I aimed to address in this book:

- What is the capacity to care and why does it matter?
- How is it acquired? What are its origins in the early development of self and morality?
- Are women better at caring than men and, if so, is this likely to change with contemporary changes in parenting and gender relations? What would constitute a good-enough family, as opposed to good-enough mothering?
- How does the capacity to care inform the ethics of care debate about relationality and autonomy and their gender?
- How do people care across distance and difference?

In this short chapter, I shall try to summarise the answers, or at least the approaches, that I have developed. I shall start with the second question, work through the successive arguments in the book (which don't exactly correspond to chapters) and then return to the first question at the end.

Self, morality and acquiring the capacity to care

How is the capacity to care acquired? What are its origins in the early development of self and morality?

Chapter 3 is about the kind of dynamic unconscious intersubjectivity (based on conflict and embodied non-symbolic communication processes) that characterises early infant–mother relations. This is the ground on which a person's self develops. An infant's psychological well-being depends on the mother's auxiliary ego and those of other familiar, primary carers. The manner in which separation and differentiation is achieved is crucial in the subsequent capacity to care of this infant. Klein's concept of the depressive position has been influential in the accounts of a number of theorists of self development on whom I have drawn. The most important principle that I extract from these theorists is that the vicissitudes of the baby's early relationships result in a permanent, dynamic tension between intersubjectivity and individuality. The latter refers to relational experiences based on differentiation between self and others and is based on the bodily experience of being separate (the 'skin ego'), whereas intersubjectivity is based on the unsymbolised forms of communication originating in the early indivisible unit (from the infant's point of view) of mother and baby, which are never expunged from the psyche. Both these facets of self, oscillating in tension, are necessary parts of the capacity to care. At best they afford accurate identification which is constantly resourced afresh by learning creatively from experience. At the same time, splitting defences, omnipotence and the desire for control are never far away when the self is threatened.

The early dyadic unit is surrounded by further complex dynamics that affect the mother's experience and, through her, the infant's. Soon the baby begins to participate in these directly rather than through the mother's psyche. I introduced useful analytical approaches for understanding how triangular relations with parents, sibling relations and perhaps group relations contribute in important ways to the formation of subjectivity. Although subsequent events and relations never stop modifying subjectivity, the early foundations of individuality and intersubjectivity have profound consequences affecting the capacity to care.

It should be clear from this account that the capacity to care cannot be assumed. It is neither natural nor given in direct ways from social circumstances. When approached psycho-socially, its fragility is evident: it is highly vulnerable to the care within which selves are forged. This raises the question of how care is changing as a result of macro-social processes such as individualisation and how these are mediated through the psycho-social processes that characterise the developmental achievement of capacity to care. The implication of my perspective is that, if subjectivity is seen as an ongoing creative tension between intersubjective processes and those producing and reproducing individuality ('feeling for others'/'feeling for me'), different social arrangements will facilitate a variety of balances and expressions of these. This is different from saying that individualisation produces more autonomous (self-reliant, less related) individuals because this implies that intersubjectivity is optional, can be lost with historical development. Rather, I am suggesting that the selves that emerge in settings affected by individualisation have found different expressions and balances of individuality and subjectivity. Narcissism, for example, is not simply an expression of individuality but is profoundly dependent on unconscious intersubjective dynamics.

The capacity to care does not stop developing with the early experiences of self that are evident in babies. The way I have incorporated later developments is by considering subsequent developmental moments in the lifespan, notably the development of gendered and maternal/parental subjectivity. As well as raising questions about the gender of parenting that are politically salient, this enabled me to modify an account of social change that is based on the assumption that individual and social group care practices can be read off from the contemporary social forces that surround them. Of course, these are influential but my argument has been that they are significantly modified by intersubjective intergenerational transmission;

that is, accomplished through transgenerational identifications. The implication is that the capacity to care contains echoes (for better or worse) of the practices that characterised earlier generations within specific communities and families. This means that cultures and families within which the care of children has been compromised can have effects lasting much longer than a single generation, effects that cannot be cancelled out only by improvements in external resources. To illustrate this argument, I have used the detailed example of men's capacity to care to consider how structural changes in parenting could affect the capacity to care of subsequent generations of boys.

Families, good-enough parenting and changing gender relations

Are women better at caring than men and, if so, is this likely to change with contemporary changes in parenting and gender relations? What would constitute a good-enough family, as opposed to good-enough mothering?

In general, women's particular positions in relation to the care of children have forged capacities to care different from men's. This has, of course, been greatly influenced by social arrangements and socially available positions, which until recently have been sharply gender differentiated. But, I have argued, it has also been due to the maternal experience of containing life beyond oneself, starting before birth in the case of the biological mother. The infant's dependency, combined with its lack of a self, demands – and usually calls forth – aspects of maternal subjectivity, profoundly based on bodily experience, that are characterised by the kind of radical intersubjectivity I have described. The experience of early mothering thus calls up the vestiges of the mother's own early intersubjectivity, which requires a new set of tensions and balances in her experience of herself. If the tension between intersubjectivity and individuality is a characteristic of recursive self formation throughout life, then different times and events in life will affect the balance achieved. Becoming a mother is the situation that demands most of the kind of unconscious communication I have described through Bion's concept of containment. If the maternal subject is the biological mother, the immediacy of embodied intersubjectivity in the experience of pregnancy, birth and breastfeeding will give unconscious communication an added foundation (potentially threatening to individuality as well as pleasurable).

To the extent that embodied intersubjectivity is involved in the capacity to care – and it is particularly important in the care of infants – then mothers are at an advantage. However, passionate involvement across the developing boundaries of the infant other and self can also put these same mothers at a disadvantage. How can they preserve a sense of themselves as different and individuated? To what extent had they achieved this before maternity? The questions posed apply in distinctly different ways across cultures because of the huge variations in women's freedoms from oppression. In different ways, however, a mother's individuality will always be present as a dynamic in relation to a child who is finding out how to separate. A person – man or woman – who is not the mother will potentially have easier access to differentiated ways of relating to the child. However, this statement too has to be qualified by recognising the ways that unconscious fantasies will affect parents' actual position; for example, leading to powerful identifications that resemble those of the biological mother. The more differentiated position will also have potential advantages and disadvantages depending on the make-up of that person: advantages of recognising the child from a position as subject in their own right and withstanding the infant's omnipotence; disadvantages if their differentiation is coloured by defences that prevent accurate identification. None of these dynamics is determined or fixed: every carer's position expresses his or her own unique balance of intersubjectivity and individuality where social and biological differences are creatively modified through unconscious fantasies.

Maternal subjectivity is distinct from the mother in two important ways. First, what the infant calls forth can be met by non-mothers and so change them in the ways that I have described. Second, the effects of good-enough maternal care are not just limited to practices within the maternal role but reconstitute her subjectivity. The capacity to care produced in mothers within this third space can extend to other thirds, creating changes in others' subjectivities. My discussion of maternal development showed the importance of the changes that take place in maternal subjectivity as children separate; changes that are likely to be most appropriate to other caring relationships.

I have described the different trajectories of boys during the demanding phase when they are both separating from their mothers and coming to terms with what is lost as a result of the recognition that they have to become boys and men. I argued that the different strategies characteristic of depressive or paranoid–schizoid coping – renunciation or repudiation – will have effects not only on the way their gendered selves develop but on their later capacity to care as parents. I also discussed how this central dynamic would be mediated by a complex of factors to do with the internal and external parents and the wider family dynamics and other circumstances such as availability.

I concluded that change towards non-gendered parenting arrangements is not likely to result in the erasure of gender difference, and certainly not in a single generation. This has to do with the infant's experience of the mother's body, the unconscious fantasy of maternal omnipotence, the father as the third term, as well as the second second, in the infant's dawning awareness of self and others and therefore the father's, or paternal subject's, significance in separation that is distinct from the mother's role in the child's separation. However, these powerful intersubjective dynamics in families are not sealed off from the real conditions of parenting and child care, whose influence works not directly by constructing subjectivity but mediated by the workings of the inner-world processes that I have described. To illustrate this, I discussed in particular the effects of cross-sex and cross-gender identifications; the way these change at different phases of the child's self development and the importance of the identificatory capacities of the parents in response.

A good-enough family does not have to be structured in the conventional gendered and hetero-normative way to provide the desirable variety of these resources; for containment, differentiation, identification and accurate recognition. Plurality is likely to maximise these resources. Triangular space seems to be crucial for the development of reflexivity. As the capacity to care depends on the ability to imagine oneself in someone else's shoes (while still having one's feet on the ground, as Winnicott put it) and symbolise the difference between me and that other (or those others), triangular relations are clearly important. This applies also to sibling and peer-group relations, which have the added crucial characteristic of being lateral and not vertical. The familiarity and trust afforded by continuity and stability in these relationships is particularly useful in childhood but I believe it applies throughout life. It is risky and difficult to allow intersubjective encounters to modify one's subjectivity without a basis in trust and this could easily be misplaced without knowledge established over time.

The capacity to care and ethical subjectivity

How does my analysis of the capacity to care inform the ethics of care debate about relationality and autonomy and their gender?

In reviewing the relevant literature in Chapter 2, I identified a crucial conceptual problem located in the dualism of connectedness–relatedness and autonomy–separation. This meant that the inevitable relatedness of caring could not cast off the taint that relatedness and care were at the expense of individuality, self expression and in a sense therefore freedom. Gilligan's and others' findings about loss of voice exemplified this issue. An adolescent girl's loss of voice is not an intrapsychic process but an intersubjective dynamic; the girl's and boy's conflicts dovetailing. I argued that the girl's residual undifferentiation and lack of separation in relation to her parents (until this point probably less defensively resolved than the boy's) will likely be transferred on to the new lateral relationship, where she loses touch with her own autonomous desires. For the boy, the more repudiated his earlier desires for maternal care, the more likely they are to be transferred on to the new, lateral relationship, still associated with the earlier omnipotent desire to control the caring feminine object on whom he depended. Perhaps friendship relations across sex, which are much more common than a generation ago, are relatively free from these dynamics.

The argument for the gendering of autonomy and connectedness in men and women, respectively, follows a similar pattern. Masculine autonomy that is the product of defensive modes of organisation, inflected by paranoid–schizoid splitting and projection, needs to be differentiated from what I have referred to as 'being a subject in one's own right'. The distinction has similarities with Keller's between static and dynamic autonomy. Although I have used this idea when referring to women's subjectivity, it is equally appropriate in the case of men; only that they are more likely to face the challenge from a position of defensive autonomy as opposed to not sufficiently differentiated connectedness. There are signs (Layton 2004) that women's access to formerly masculine positions and institutional settings is producing character structures in women based on defensive autonomy. It is further evidence that such subjectivities are gendered, rather than sexed. It is clearly important for feminism that women's struggles for independence need not and should not be based on masculine autonomy but on being subjects in their own right – to which men can likewise aspire. This does not in principle conflict with an ethic of care; indeed, good 'caring about' requires this differentiated subjectivity.

One concern in my account of self development and the capacity to care has been to explain and describe how the binary between autonomy and connectedness can be transcended and how in practice good care not only can involve subject–subject relations but may depend on them. Differentiation, a necessary feature of psychological separation, is required for the transformation of what is often called 'overidentification' into accurate identification. My account of unconscious inter-subjectivity is central here to a description of caring about as an example of tolerating the tension between experiencing the other's needs and one's own difference.

The theoretical account that I have developed to incorporate both the inter-subjectivity and individuality of subjectivity draws on Thomas Ogden's dialectical model of the third which is 'a creation of the first two who are also created by it' (Ogden 1994/1999: 462). Subjectivity is not either autonomous or connected: it is both, but not in a simply additive fashion. The 'third' conceptualises how these come together in a recurrent dynamic way produced out of internal conflict or tension that modifies the former constellation of subjectivity, 'the experience of being simultaneously within and outside of the intersubjectivity' (Ogden 1994: 64).

Ogden's account emphasises the creative modifications that can be produced intersubjectively in the third space, but modifications resulting from defensive encounters are less clear. Here Bion's account of the different intersubjective processes that produce openness of thinking to new experiences (+K) and defensive closure of thinking (–K) was useful in understanding gender differences in moral reasoning and how they are potentially reflected in care practices. According to Klein, Winnicott and Alford, concern, compassion, gratitude and reparation (all aspects of the capacity to care) are closely bound up with the depressive as opposed to the paranoid–schizoid form of psychic organisation. Boys, in particular, may cope with the threats associated with loss of identifications with good caring objects associated with the mother through repudiation. This is not only likely to lead to splitting off and projecting care into the feminine other, but to forms of thinking based on residual omnipotence and desire to control the external world through instrumental reason. Such channels have been far more accessible to Western boys than girls (through discursive positions and masculine identifications). Alford contrasted instrumental reason with the reparative reason of the depressive position, which he linked to caritas.

125

Caring across distance and difference

How do people care across distance and difference?

The basis of all 'caring about' is the movement between individuality and inter-subjectivity that is a continuous core of human relating. On the face of it, this statement is consistent with Levinas' ethics; the 'interhuman order' and the conflict involved in an unconditional response to the other's suffering. However, I argued that his lack of particularity about real others in his concept of the Other, and the lack in his account of relationships of the kind of dynamic unconscious intersubjectivity that crosses the boundaries of individual selves, resulted in a failure to explain ethical relations. I wanted to provide an account of how these were achieved, to supplement the abstract nature of Levinas' commandment of unconditional responsibility for the Other.

The mother–child paradigm of care has frequently been connected with an 'over-identified', suffocating style of care and this has encouraged the use of a friendship model based on assumptions of equality and reciprocity. I modified this critique with an account of how maternal development, along with every child's need to separate, moves out of the dyadic mode of asymmetrical dependency and power, potentially into a reciprocal capacity to care between people who are both subjects in their own right. Friendship is arguably better protected from the dangers of care relations motivated by omnipotence expressed in the wish to control the other through their dependence on care. This could be due to the distance in the transference – particularly for the men's friendships on which the model was built – from the vertical mother–infant experience to the lateral ones, informed by sibling relationships. Transferences are powered by unconscious fantasies however and are not constrained by objective age and sex difference, so care in friendship is not freely invented but prefigured by earlier relationships, albeit with new characteristics.

The capacity to give and receive care in a fluid interchangeable and reciprocal way, depending on the ebb and flow of needs and circumstances is surprisingly rare. The lateral relations of siblinghood affect care among friends, affecting the character of both intersubjectivity and individuality, for example dynamics that enhance mutual recognition such as sharing the same experiences, the sameness of each sibling's position in relation to the parents, rivalry and their potential for joining forces against parental authority. Even in same-sex, same-age, same-ethnicity relationships free from gender and generational and racialised divisions of care, splitting of care-giving and care-receiving is commonplace. Power should not just be conceptualised sociologically as a product of social and structural differences. Viewed psycho-socially, power is motivated by conflicts to do with desire for omnipotent control and recognition. These combine with structural power and make power relations in care more complex and less predictable. In freely chosen relationships, each can still be invested in the different kinds of power entailed in these positions, unsettled only perhaps by dramatic impingements from outside.

126

'Caring about' flourishes or is compromised in different ways as a result of early primary relationships and the way these extend across the lifespan and across various forms of group, community, institution and network, supported or undermined by practices and discourses that have implications for care. I chose the reform in children's hospital wards in 1950s London as an example both of the power of institutional policy, practice and dominant discourses to produce care that is not good enough and to show how individuals can exercise caring agency that transcends those constraints. Robertson, with the help of the new attachment discourse, was able to identify with the suffering of young hospitalised children across several potentially othering dimensions of social distance. He enabled others to identify through the use of a visual medium of representation and the particularity of an individual case.

The use of particularity and visual representation is widespread in attempts to get people to care across gulfs of distance and difference. The success of these attempts depends on the viewer's capacity for identification, through introjection, that has its roots in the enduring unconscious intersubjectivity that is part of subjectivity. Identification is not a magic bullet of 'caring about', however. Like all psychodynamic processes, it comes in a variety of forms that I represented on a continuum of accuracy. Accurate-enough identification involves learning something in the moment about that particular other, a capacity that involves having an emotional experience (this is what makes it meaningful). In each such emotional experience, intersubjectivity meets individuality and, to the extent that it is capable of symbolisation, results in a reality check, so that simultaneously I can know the difference between my situation and yours, between me and you. The combination enables accurate-enough recognition of the needs of particular others in the context of one's capacity to meet those needs. This account overcomes the problem, frequently discussed in feminist literatures on care ethics, about over-identification or empathy and its likely ill effects on caring about. It also recognises limits to the accuracy of recognition across difference without the practical involvement that produces learning by experience.

Whereas charity, caritas and the ethics of care have frequently been understood as features of intimate, face-to-face relations and of the private sphere, the understanding of care across distance and difference poses the question of how care contributes to justice ethics and informs citizenship and rights. I used the question posed by Dobson: 'what motivates the universal obligation of cosmopolitanism whose principles cover the relations between all human beings?' My answer again depended on the idea of identification, specifically identification with differences. Specificity is helpful in enabling identification, through universal common experiences, ultimately life and death, safety, satisfaction and suffering. These provide the vitality – the concern – which can transform abstract principles of justice into practical justice.

The capacity to care and why it matters

What is the capacity to care and why does it matter?

The capacity to care underpins 'caring about', which, in Sevenhuijsen's words (2002: 10), is the 'heart and soul' of care. It is crucial to the application of an ethic of care in private, public and global life. I have said that the capacity to care ideally includes four facets when expressed in practice:

1. The capacity to provide the non-negotiable, asymmetrical demand for maternal care.
2. The capacity for reciprocal interdependent care receiving and care giving.
3. The capacity for self care.
4. The capacity for extended care to both human and non-human objects outside direct experience.

Early maternal care – non-negotiable, asymmetrical – is, I have argued, a prototype for the capacity to care. This is because the experience of this care (good enough or not) creates the floor of everyone's self and lies at the heart of all dependency and all care receiving as well as care giving. The care relationship is held in our bodily memories, known but unsymbolised; there as a resource for all future encounters. This resource derives from the intersubjectivity that characterises the early encounters with care and remains with us throughout life. It starts at a time when there is no distinction between infant and carer, when the mother's psyche is the infant's psyche, when communication is achieved without symbolisation through introjection and projection. It is the ground on which identifications are built. Early maternal care (by which I mean something wider than care given by mothers) is the warp on which individuality is woven and produces the themes on which later subjectivity, including capacity to care, is founded.

Reciprocal symmetrical care, characteristic – ideally – of equals, depends on a transformation from ruthless demand for care from an object experienced narcissistically as an extension of one's desires to being a subject in one's own right, the converse of which is being able to recognise the other as such a subject. In short, we can call these 'subject–subject' relations. The capacity to sustain these is neither easy nor once-for-all-time. The conflicts of differentiation and recognition, individuality and intersubjectivity, omnipotence and respect for the other as subject, difference and sameness, splitting and acceptance of good and bad in the same object; all will infuse reciprocal relations of care and inform relations across social power differences, enabling them to be creative and drawing on different meanings of sibling and parental relationships through transference.

Self care is not just the opposite of necessary dependence on others for care; it is also the opposite of self harm. Self harm occurs when feelings of self worth are fragile or inaccessible; a situation that results from lack of the kind of care from others that conveys that you are of value by being who you are and doing what you do. I have argued that self care and other care are not mutually exclusive sides of subjectivity but mutually enhancing. When they are in conflict, it is in the context of the mundane constraints of life. If a person is well differentiated, he or she is in a position to learn to recognise his or her own self worth through accurate recognition, for which we depend on others. This in turn should encourage self care rather than self harm.

If the capacity to care has its origins in the first, bodily, intimate relations with continuous carers, then the question of if and how this extends to caring about different and distant others assumes political importance. Identifications do in practice work to enable the experience of others' well-being and suffering beyond humans to animals and – as is evident from their important role in many religions – to other natural objects. Identifications can be both unsymbolised and symbolised, and the way that the unsymbolised achieves symbolic expression is crucial in the capacity to care. As self conscious ethical subjects, we focus on what is capable of symbolisation (by definition, what we are aware of); what is expressible through language, organised discursively. I have concentrated on the unsymbolised intersubjective channels such as introjection because these go unrecognised and misrecognised in the understanding of care. Discourses pre-exist individuals and enable the symbolisation of what is introjected, influencing the meaning that is achieved. But that meaning is also achieved through the creative imagination that characterises the internal world.

Caring across distance, when it is in addition to difference, may be reduced by this inability to learn by practical, direct experience and the desire to control the world through understanding and the abstract application of higher order principles. But defensive abstract thinking is not a necessary feature of justice, which can be brought to life by specificity and the channel this affords for identifications.

The capacity to care matters because, without it, society would not survive. Neither would individuals survive, except perhaps as heartless and soulless psychopaths, existing physically in a world made terrifying by a lack of trust born out of and reproduced by failure of care. The capacity to care needs to be protected: it cannot be taken for granted and what is more, its feminine intergenerational transmission can no longer be relied upon in an individualising world where gender relations have been transformed. Changes in gender relations pose a threat to the old order of care but offer the opportunity of a new one. In this new order, care need not be limited to the maternal, or the domestic, but can underpin citizenship, public institutions and work. It can extend to the domains of justice ethics. This also means an order where the maternal is not limited to women and a gender order where women's capacities to care are not an expression of prohibitions that make it impossible to be subjects in their own right.

If, as I have argued, psycho-social transformation of care through changing gender relations is a more complicated, less direct and less malleable proposition than the assumptions contained in social models of change, there are implications for policy. Certainly, child care is crucial, as is the support of diverse kinds of families. I hope that the desirable quality of this care can be better grasped as a result of my account of the subjectivity that underpins the capacity to care, whose acquisition depends on those capacities in primary carers. These capacities are little understood and undervalued in instrumental cultures based on a myth of rational autonomous subjectivity where ethical life is understood as a set of principles to be followed. My account of caring subjectivity is radically different: a dialectical movement of intersubjectivity and individuality in which accurate identifications with the experience of specific others and the conditions of their lives are capable of symbolisation and thereby generalisation and pervade all the relations that make up an ethical life.

AFTERWORD

In the book's introduction (Chapter 1), I stated that in problematising the assumption that the capacity to care is natural, I also wanted to challenge the notion that it is simply social; historically and culturally variable and the socialised result of habit, training or practice. This goal to go beyond the dualism of biological individual versus social causes is consistent with the psycho-social perspective that, as a feminist and critical social psychologist, I have been committed to. It has required a serious engagement with psychoanalysis as the means to include a genuinely psychological level of understanding. The effect of the binary has been to squeeze out psychology and thus leave social discourses of care without a theory of the caring subject, vulnerable to the seduction of a 'natural' capacity to care.

A psycho-social account of the capacity to care is not only difficult in the context of a pervasive legacy of dualism but it is dangerous in the context of social and feminist approaches that are prone to treat all psychology with suspicion (not without historical justification). Feminism's commitment to the sharing of childcare has been one of its central platforms since the start of second-wave feminism, accompanied by downplaying the significance of women's capacity to give birth for their psychology and their subsequent parenting. Having participated in these tendencies, I have also had to come to terms with my doubts; fuelled by my own experience of mothering, certainly, but also by my theoretical inquiries.

It seems relevant, therefore, to put my arguments in this book in the perspective of their historical and political trajectory in order to pre-empt a reading of it as unmindful of the critiques of psychological accounts that have played such an important part in feminist and social science debates. It is in the context and aftermath of these debates that I have arrived at the views outlined in this book. For example, it was not until the final draft of this book (and it went through many) that I came to terms with using the concept of 'individuality' in tandem with the principle of 'unconscious intersubjectivity'. Until that point I thought that the principle of unconscious intersubjectivity would suffice to go beyond the dualism of the autonomous individual and connected subject-in-relation. In retrospect I understand this blind spot to be influenced by the critique of the 'individual' of psychology in which I participated as a member of the group who wrote *Changing the subject* (Henriques *et al*. 1984).

131

The treatment of psychological processes is not the only difficulty that I have encountered as a result of the various critical turns that characterised social science in the final decades of the twentieth century. The other, related, critique involved shunning the realism that characterised science (including social science) accounts in favour of a post-structuralist or post-modern emphasis on mediation, construction and broadly on the impossibility of knowing reality (summed up by the capital T in Foucault's concept of Truth). My position in this book is realist: real care, real effects of mothering, real changes in the child in the process of becoming. However – again as a result of my formation during the critical turn – this realism is tempered and I call it critical realism. This means that I am trying to theorise the effects of real circumstances and real relationships through the grid of how these achieve meaning. And meaning is not just achieved through the availability of certain discourses and practices rather than others, but through the mediations of psychic processes, themselves inextricably captured by language, but also by phantasy, anxiety and desire. In this respect too, my approach is psycho-social and also critical realist. The dualism of relativism and realism is as difficult to negotiate as that between the individual and the social. When I am talking about mothering, am I referring to mothering discourse or the real thing? And how can the latter be separated from the former? The same goes for the baby or child. Can I see through discourses of children to real children? How? When am I dealing with one and when the other? Or how do I treat them if the object of my analysis is inextricably both? Many social science books remain on the territory of discourse but I am interested in subjectivity (in this respect I continue to be a psychologist at heart) and I did not want to write a book about care discourses or even about constructions in the literature of the capacity to care. The purpose of addressing the latter is to navigate a critical way through them in order to provide a way of understanding the capacity to care in its myriad manifestations. I hope I have to some extent succeeded without unintentionally reproducing uncritical discourses that distort or oppress in their treatment of babies, children, mothers, fathers and other significant carers; indeed all the figures in this book behind which are actual people whose ethical subjectivities bear the marks of others' capacities to care and are expressed through their own.

NOTES

CHAPTER 1

1 It is worth qualifying this assertion by saying that the claim does not work in reverse: not all those who have suffered traumatic failures of care turn out to damage others. Some damage themselves. Some transcend their experiences through the creative use of internal resources that somehow survived the damage.

2 Elisabeth Badinter (1981) furnished rich historical material that seemed to suggest that the many parents in late eighteenth-century Paris who farmed out their infants for wet nursing did so without much solicitude.

3 See *Feminism and psychology*, 12 (1) (2002) for an evaluation, nearly 25 years on.

4 Care writers in the feminist philosophy tradition such as Bowden (1997), Friedman (1993) and Card (1996) have addressed this binary, but they have not addressed the question of the model of self and self development that could transcend it.

5 Modified, these then formed part of a model of the 'elements' of care which, combined with the 'phases' of care, came out as: caring about – attentiveness; caring for – responsibility; taking care of – competence and care receiving – responsiveness.

6 Sevenhuijsen typically adds trust to the qualities of care that she drew from Tronto; trust that she sees as the 'oil in the wheel of care' (2003: 15).

7 For example, see Bell 1993, Card 1996, Hoagland 1991.

CHAPTER 2

1 This is the case in philosophy and social theory (*Hypatia* 10(2) 1995; Roseneil and Hogan (eds) 2001; Hogan and Roseneil (eds) 2003; *Feminist theory* vols 2(2) and 4(2)), in politics (Sevenhuijsen 1998), social policy (Williams 2004) and psychology (Larabee 1993).

2 I use the two terms 'relational subjectivity' and 'intersubjectivity' in slightly different contexts in this book. The impossibility of settling on one or the other reflects the varying uses of both terms in the relevant literatures and, more importantly, the fact that my central paradigm is based on the coexistence, in permanent creative tension, of differentiated subjectivity and intersubjectivity.

3 Dorothy Dinnerstein in 1976 and Elisabeth Badinter (1981), in a French intellectual tradition, concluded likewise.

4 Hekman (1999: 93) maintains that, in her writings, Gilligan was consistent in her refusal to valorise the ethic of care above an ethic of justice. In practice, however, her work with girls treated their care ethic as wholly desirable and the effect of her work has certainly been to valorise women's relationality and its expression in an ethic of care above that of an ethic of justice. Other feminist figures advocating an ethic of care, notably Joan Tronto and Virginia Held, conclude that it is superior (see Hekman

1999: 93). The source for this debate is a special issue of *Hypatia* (1995), 10(2) based on an American symposium on care and justice.

5 'By voice I mean something like what most people mean when they speak of the core of the self . . . Speaking and listening are a form of psychic breathing . . . a litmus test of relationships and a measure of psychological health' (Gilligan 1993: xvi).

6 Lynn Phillips' (2000) account of her empirical work with young North American women in heterosexual relationships is powerful evidence of this tendency, despite decades of feminism. See also Benjamin (1998).

7 Critiques of an integrated self have come from psychoanalysis (especially Lacan), and feminist postmodernism's emphasis on multiple and fragmented subjectivity (for example, Butler 1990, 2004).

8 The primary location of this work is Jordan *et al.* (1991). They are also referred to as the Stone Center.

9 Alford (1989) argues that the Frankfurt school's uncritical adoption of this Freudian position contradicted its overall aims and in particular their critique of instrumental rationality.

10 'One of the greatest weaknesses in many feminist analyses of gender issues has been their tendency to undervalue the potency of unconscious motivations' (Flax 1990: 398).

11 In Britain, women therapists at the London Women's Therapy Centre addressed the issue of women's identity development in the mother–daughter relationship through their work with women (Eichenbaum and Orbach 1983, Ernst 1987).

12 In Freudian psychoanalysis, the ego consists of the organised parts of the self that govern rational thought and action. The superego derives from parental introjects and enables self-criticism. It is often thought to be a punitive part of the self, the location of a moral voice.

13 Nonetheless, Gilligan's (1982) work with adult women reasoning about the ethical dilemmas surrounding abortion suggests similarly that women are still largely exhibiting care, rather than justice reasoning, that is basing their reasoning on specific, relational knowledge that they can extrapolate from their own experience.

14 This distinction is still consistent with Butler's (2004: 9) reminder that "'anatomy' and 'sex' are not without their cultural framing".

15 This concept is discussed at greater length in Chapter 3. In brief, projective identification, in the context of Bion's usage, refers to the unconscious projection of a state of mind into an object (another person) and identifying it there. It achieves the purposes of communicating one's mental state and also of evacuating what is hard to tolerate. 'Excessive projection', according to Bion, referred to excess of belief in one's omnipotence (Bion 1962a: 114, cited in Hinshelwood 1991: 184).

16 I mean objectivity in the psychoanalytic sense, and not in the positivist sense (Fox Keller 1985 chapter 6, Hollway 2000).

17 The experimental setting for the 'Heinz dilemma' calls into question how Jake and Amy made sense of their task. Nonetheless, they and the others were both in the same situation and the patterning of differences calls for some explanation.

CHAPTER 3

1 In this chapter I use 'mother' to denote the primary carer, from birth onwards. In Chapter 4 and again in Chapter 6, I raise questions about what 'primary' carer might mean when performed by different people, the biological mother, the father or other person.

2 Waddell (1998: 42 footnote 1) clarifies that because Klein used 'breast' as an 'emblem for intimacy' the quality of intimacy was important and not the issue of whether the infant was fed with breast or bottle.

3 Hate is only the opposite of love. 'Hate would not exist if love were not present' (Bion 1962b: 10). It encompasses milder emotions like dislike, irritation, anger and the wish to reject. Yet in our culture it is regarded as too strong and many people wish to reject the idea rather than think about it. This can be seen as a defence against anxiety operating at a discursive level and reproduced through unconscious dynamics. Kleinian psychoanalysis, in insisting on the coexistence of love and hate, was making a point about the primitive character of emotions in unconscious life, emotions that are likely to be defended against.

4 The parallel dynamic is when the bad is retained in order to protect the good by projecting it out on to the object. This leads to the phenomenon of idealising the other and denigrating oneself. But I am jumping ahead to how these states of mind manifest later in life.

5 I shall return to the important issue of the capacity for identification when self boundaries are nonetheless clear and therefore the parties are differentiated (Chapter 6). It is an issue whose confusion has undermined progress in the feminist debates about autonomy and connectedness (see Chapter 2).

6 Primary narcissism, in Freudian terminology, refers to 'the love of self which precedes loving others' (Rycroft 1972: 94). Klein thought in terms of narcissistic states 'in which there is a retreat to a mental state in which omnipotent phantasies of identification come to the fore' (Hinshelwood 1991: 356). This is characteristic of the paranoid–schizoid position. A distinction is usually made between the 'libidinal and destructive aspects of narcissism' (Rosenfeld 1971: 173, cited in Hinshelwood 1991: 358).

7 These two concepts should not be regarded as synonymous: it is possible to have separation without differentiation, notably when it is accomplished in defensive mode.

8 In patriarchal cultures where unequal (unfair) treatment of boys and girls is formalised and deeply set in family practices, it is surely here, in childhood sibling relations, that the meanings of justice and injustice become etched into subjectivity and its gendered expression.

CHAPTER 4

1 Raphael-Leff (2003) (Ed) explores in detail how parental subjectivity involves the reworking of previously undigested experiences from parents' own childhoods.

2 Birth is increasingly questioned as the starting point of experience, now that new technologies can show what goes on inside the womb. Using ultrasound technology and following up babies for a year or more after birth, Piontelli (1992) found powerful evidence of the effects of fetal experience on subsequent personality.

3 This qualification is what turns a socio-cultural approach into a psycho-social approach.

4 Ogden also calls this the 'analytic third' because it emerges out of his understanding of the clinical psychoanalytic relationship, but as I shall apply it in a non-analytic context, I will use his shorter label.

5 Bion's memoir suggests that he provided this while an officer in the trenches of the First World War, extending care to frightened young men in conditions of terror (Bion 1982).

6 Similarly, Winnicott understood creativity to be located in a transitional space that drew from external reality but was not limited by it.

7 'Going on being' is a Winnicottian phrase that Ogden points out is particularly apt because it does not identify a subject or object, whether that is mother or child (Ogden 2001: 227).

8 The unconscious preparation does not just happen in pregnancy. For example, one twenty-year-old woman, free from commitments and not in a heterosexual relationship, told me that she dreamt that she went out to a club and then remembered that she had

left her new baby in a drawer back at her student house. She thought that it might be dead and phoned a housemate to go and look after it.

9   To be more specific, these are psycho-social processes, in the sense that they continue to be forged in the intersubjective third that exists between mother and child.

10 Whereas 'fantasy' is the usual spelling, Klein used 'phantasy' to designate unconscious fantasies. My spelling reflects these usages.

11 In my experience of organisational dynamics and occupying managerial positions, I have become convinced that such maternal transferences, especially from younger colleagues of both sexes, continue to have effects on the way that women exercise power and authority and on its reception in organisational hierarchies. These are not necessarily negative.

12 Mothers may not manage this balancing act if they have been too damaged as a result of previous relationships; for example, see Maynes and Best (1997).

13 Winnicott described the paradox in his inimitably down-to-earth style in referring to the analyst's job: 'to stand in the patient's shoes from a position, that is, of having his own feet on the ground' (Winnicott 1958, cited in Khan's introduction to Winnicott 1975a: xxvii).

CHAPTER 5

1   'Three in five working mothers would stay at home with their children if they could afford to, a poll suggests. Of those in work, only 12% said they wanted to pursue a challenging career whereas 60% said they were only back at work because of financial commitments.' This BBC news report, on 6 February 2004, refers to the results of a British poll.

2   This is an oversimplification: Winnicott described the relationship as follows: 'I have come to compare external reality not so much with fantasy as with an inner reality . . . it is part of one's manic defence to be unable to give full significance to inner reality. Fantasy is part of the individual's effort to deal with inner reality . . . the individual gets to external reality through the omnipotent fantasies elaborated in the effort to get away from inner reality' (Cited in Khan's introduction to Winnicott 1975a: xiii, from a 1935 paper).

3   Benjamin's periodisation of early gender development has four main phases: nominal gender identification; early differentiation of identifications in the context of separation–individuation; the pre-Oedipal overinclusive phase and the Oedipal phase (1995: 53).

4   There is a great deal of clinical and research evidence to suggest that boys whose fathers are emotionally unavailable fare less well as they are growing up. 'The number of patients in psychoanalytic therapy whose fathers (whether due to abandonment or death) disappeared during childhood appears to be greater than that found in the population at large' (McDougall 1993: 239).

5   Etchegoyen, taking her cue from Winnicott's aphorism about there being no such thing as a baby, states 'There is no such thing as a father without the mother's relationship to the father' (2002: 34).

6   At this age 'Separation consists not so much of losing mother's presence but losing control of her coming and going' (Benjamin 1994: 134).

7   Margaret Mahler described rapprochement as a phase involved in the baby's separation–individuation conflicts. It centres on the baby's struggle (starting at about fourteen months) to face the distinction between what she can do herself and what she depends on her mother to do. Reframed by Benjamin to reflect her intersubjective emphasis, it can be defined as 'the crisis of recognizing the other – specifically of confronting mother's independence' (Benjamin 1995: 37). Traditionally, the father has

represented the possibility of independence and Benjamin distinguishes this from the Oedipal turn to the father, which is much later.

CHAPTER 6

1 We saw in Chapter 5 the conditions that made it likely for boys to follow this trajectory.
2 For example, in the case of women in the developing world who leave behind their own children to earn money by caring for children or dependent adults in the developed world (Ehrenreich and Hochschild 2002), the capacity to care for, and recognise the dependence of, their employers suggests the continuing tension of the power relations in recognition rather than their breakdown into monolithic domination.
3 The capitalised Other indicates a universal philosophical category that suffers in certain contexts from being stripped of its specificity. For this reason I have used 'other', which can include specific others whose own responses are crucial in their effects.
4 Abelin thought it was only after about 18 months that a baby was aware of the mother and father's relationship (1980).
5 From a group dynamic perspective, the large group 'exaggerates the goodness and badness of the abstractions with which it deals' (Alford 1989: 57).

REFERENCES

Abelin, E. (1975) Some further observations and comments on the earliest role of the father. *International Journal of Psychoanalysis*, 56, 293–302.

Abelin, E. (1980) Triangulation, the role of the father, and the origins of core gender identity during the rapprochement subphase. In R.F. Lax, S. Bach and J.A. Burland (Eds), *Rapprochement* (pp. 151–170). New York: Aronson.

Ainsworth, M., Bell, D. and Stayton, D. (1974) Infant-mother attachment and social development. In M. Richards (Ed.), *The integration of a child into a social world* (pp. 99–136). Cambridge: Cambridge University Press.

Ainsworth, M., Blehar, M.C., Waters, E. and Wall, S. (1978) *Patterns of attachment*. Hillsdale, NJ: Lawrence Erlbaum Associates.

Alford, F. (1989) *Melanie Klein and critical social theory*. New Haven, CT: London: Yale University Press.

Alford, F. (2002) *Levinas, the Frankfurt School and psychoanalysis*. Middletown, CN: Wesleyan University Press.

Alizade, A. (1999) *Feminine sensuality*. London: Karnac Books.

Anzieu, D. (1985) *The skin ego*. New Haven, CT: Yale University Press.

Arendt, H. (1958) *The human condition*. Chicago: Chicago University Press.

Aristotle (1940) *Aristotle on friendship. An expanded translation of the Nichomachean ethics books VIII and IX* by Geoffrey Percival. Cambridge: Cambridge University Press.

Aron, L. (1996) *Meeting of minds*. Hillsdale, NJ: The Analytic Press.

Badinter, E. (1981) *The myth of motherhood: an historical view of the maternal instinct*. London: Souvenir Press.

Badoe, Y. (2005) *The witches of Gambaga. Report to the African Gender Institute*. Cape Town, South Africa: University of Cape Town.

Baraitser, L. (2006a) Oi mother, keep ye' hair on! Impossible transformations of maternal subjectivity. *Studies in Gender and Sexuality*, 7(3), 217–238.

Baraitser, L. (2006b) Response to 'What exactly is the transformation of motherhood?, de Marneffe's commentary on Baraitser's paper "Oi mother, keep ye' hair on! Impossible transformations of maternal subjectivity"'. *Studies in Gender and Sexuality*, 7(3), 249–257.

Bassin, D., Honey, M. and Kaplan, M.M. (Eds) (1994) *Representations of motherhood*. New Haven: Yale University Press.

Beck-Gernsheim, E. (1983/2002) From 'living for others' to 'a life of one's own'. In U.Beck and E. Beck-Gernsheim, *Individualization* (pp. 54–84). London: Sage.

Beebe, B., Lachman, F. and Jaffe, J. (1997) Mother–infant interaction structures and presymbolic self and object representation. *Psychoanalytic Dialogues*, 7, 133–182.

Bell, L. (1993) *Rethinking ethics in the midst of violence: a feminist approach to freedom.* Lanham, MD: Rowman and Littlefield.

Benjamin, J. (1978) Authority and the family revisited: or, a world without fathers? *New German Critique*, 13, 35–57.

Benjamin, J. (1984) Master and slave: the fantasy of erotic domination. In A. Snitow, C. Stansell and S. Thompson (Eds), *Desire: the politics of sexuality.* London: Virago.

Benjamin, J. (1990) *The bonds of love.* London: Virago.

Benjamin, J. (1994) The omnipotent mother: a psychoanalytic study of fantasy and reality. In D. Bassin, M. Honey and M.M. Kaplan (Eds), *Representations of motherhood* (pp. 129–146), New Haven, CT: Yale University Press.

Benjamin, J. (1995) *Like subjects, love objects – essays on recognition and sexual difference.* New Haven, CT: Yale University Press.

Benjamin, L.J. (1998) *Shadow of the other: intersubjectivity and gender in psychoanalysis.* New York: Routledge.

Benner, P. and J. Wrubel (1989) *The primacy of caring.* Menlo Park, CA: Addison-Wesley.

Bick, E. (1986) Further considerations of the function of the skin in early object relations: findings from infant observation integrated into child and adult analysis. *British Journal of Psychotherapy*, 2(4), 292–301.

Bion, W.R. (1959) Attacks on linking. *International Journal of Psychoanalysis*, 40, 308–315.

Bion, W.R. (1962a) Theory of thinking. *International Journal of Psychoanalysis*, 43, 306–310.

Bion, W.R. (1962b) *Learning from experience.* London: Maresfield.

Bion, W. R. (1967) *Second thoughts.* London: Maresfield.

Bion, W.R. (1982) *The long weekend, 1897–1919.* Abingdon: Fleetwood.

Blum, L. (1987) Particularity and responsiveness. In J. Kagan and S. Lamb (Eds), *The emergence of morality in young children.* Chicago University Press. Reprinted in Blum, L. (1994) *Moral perception and particularity.* Cambridge: Cambridge University Press.

Bollas, C. (1987) *Shadow of the object.* New York: Columbia Press.

Bollas, C. (1999) *The mystery of things.* London: Routledge.

Bot, S. and Corbasson, C. (1998) Cutting the umbilical cord: a critique of the self-in-relation theory of female psychological development from psychoanalytic perspectives. *Gender and Psychoanalysis*, 3(4), 413–433.

Bowden, P (1997) *Caring. Gender-sensitive ethics.* London: Routledge.

Bradley, B. (1989) *Visions of infancy: a critical introduction to child development.* Cambridge: Polity Press.

Bradley, B. (2006) *The origins of group-mindedness: studies of infants in groups.* Talk to the Department of Psychology, Open University. January 2006.

Bradley, B. and Selby, J. (2004) Observing infants in groups: the clan revisited. *International Journal of Infant Observation and its Applications*, 7 (2/3), 107–122.

Brannen, J., Moss, P. and Mooney, A. (2004) *Working and caring over the twentieth century: change and continuity in four-generation families.* Basingstoke: Palgrave MacMillan.

Britton, R. (1993) The missing link: parental sexuality in the Oedipus complex. In D. Breen (Ed.) *The gender conundrum* (pp. 82–94). London: Routledge.

Britton, R. (1998) *Belief and imagination.* London: Routledge.

Britton, R. (2002) Forever father's daughter: the Athene–Antigone complex. In J. Trowell and A. Etchegoyen (Eds), *The importance of fathers, a psychoanalytic re-evaluation* (pp. 107–118). Sussex, UK: Brunner-Routledge.

Broughton, J. (1993) Women's rationality and men's virtues: a critique of gender dualism in Gilligan's theory of moral development. In Larabee, M. (Ed.), *An ethic of care* (pp. 112–142). New York: Routledge.

Brown, L-M. and Gilligan, C. (1993) Meeting at the crossroads: women's psychology and girls' development. *Feminism and Psychology*, 3(1), 11–35.

Brown, N.O. (1966) *Love's body*. New York: Vintage.

Burman, E. (1994) *Deconstructing developmental psychology*. London: Routledge.

Butler, J. (1990) *Gender trouble*. New York: Routledge.

Butler, J. (2004) *Undoing gender*. New York: Routledge

Card, C. (1996) *The unnatural lottery: character and moral luck*. Philadelphia, PA: Temple University Press.

Chasseguet-Smirgel, J. (1964/1985) *Female sexuality*. London: Maresfield.

Chodorow, N. (1978) *The reproduction of mothering*. London: University of California Press.

Chodorow, N. (1989) *Feminism and psychoanalytic theory*. New Haven, CT: Yale University Press.

Chodorow, N. (2002) The cycle completed: mothers and children. *Feminism and Psychology*, 12(1), 11–17.

Chodorow, N. and Contratto, S. (1989) The fantasy of the perfect mother. In Chodorow, N., *Feminism and psychoanalytic theory* (pp. 79–96). New Haven, CT: Yale University Press.

Cohen, R.A. (2002) Maternal psyche. In E.E. Gantt and R.N. Williams (Eds), *Psychology for the other: Levinas, ethics and the practice of psychology* (pp. 32–64). Pittsburgh, PA: Duquesne University Press/Dorset: Orca.

Cohen, S. (2001) *States of denial: knowing about atrocities and suffering*, Cambridge: Polity Press.

Connolly, W.E. (2002) *Identity/difference: democratic negotiations of political paradox*. St Paul, MN: University of Minnesota Press.

Coward, R (1997) The heaven and the hell of mothering. In W. Hollway and B. Featherstone (Eds), *Mothering and ambivalence* (pp. 111–118). London: Routledge.

de Beauvoir, S. (1949/1972) *The second sex*. Harmondsworth: Penguin.

de Marneffe, D. (2004) *Maternal desire: on children, love and the inner life*. New York: Little Brown.

Diamond, N. and Marrone, M. (2003) *Attachment and intersubjectivity*. London: Whurr.

Dinnerstein, D. (1976) *The rocking of the cradle and the ruling of the world*. New York: Harper and Row.

Dobson, A. (2006) Thick cosmopolitanism. *Political Studies*, 54(1), 165–184.

Edwards, E. (2001) *Raw histories: photographs, anthropology and museums*. Oxford, Berg.

Ehrenreich, B. and Hochschild, A. (Eds) (2002) *Global women: nannies, maids and sex workers in the new economy*. London: Granta Books.

Eichenbaum, L. and Orbach, S. (1983) *What do women want?* Glasgow: Fontana/Collins.

Ernst, S. (1987) Can a daughter be a woman? Women's identity and psychological separation. In S. Ernst and M. Maguire (Eds), *Living with the Sphinx. Papers from The Women's Therapy Centre*. London: The Women's Press (pp. 68–115).

Ernst, S. (1997) Mothers and daughters within a changing world. In W. Hollway and B. Featherstone (Eds), *Mothering and ambivalence* (pp. 80–88). London: Routledge.

Etchegoyen, A. (2002) Psychoanalytic ideas about fathers. In J. Trowell and A. Etchegoyen (Eds), *The importance of fathers, a psychoanalytic re-evaluation* (pp. 20–42). Sussex, UK: Brunner-Routledge.

Everingham, C. (1994) *Motherhood and modernity*. Buckingham, UK: Open University Press.

Fakhry Davids, M. (2002) Fathers in the internal world: from boy to man to father. In J. Trowell and A. Etchegoyen (Eds), *The importance of fathers, a psychoanalytic re-evaluation* (pp. 67–92). Sussex, UK: Brunner-Routledge.

Fast, I. (1984) *Gender identity*. Hillsdale, NJ: The Analytic Press.

Ferenczi, S. (1926/1980) The problem of acceptance of unpleasant ideas – advances in knowledge of the sense of reality. In S. Ferenci, J. Rickman (compiler) and J.I. Shuttie (translator), *Further contributions to the theory and technique of psycho-analysis* (Maresfield Reprints). London: Karnac.

Fifer, W. (1980) Of human bonding: newborns prefer their mothers' voices. *Science*, 208, 1174–1176.

Firestone, S. (1970) *The dialectic of sex*. London: Jonathan Cape.

First, E. (1988) The leaving game: I'll play you and you'll play me; the emergence of the capacity for dramatic role play in two-year-olds. In A. Slade and D, Wolfe (Eds), *Modes of meaning: clinical developmental approaches to symbolic play* (pp. 32–160). New York: Oxford University Press.

Fisher, B. and Tronto, J. (1990) Towards a feminist theory of caring. In E.K. Abel and M. Nelson (Eds), *Circles of care: work and identity in women's lives* (pp. 35–62). Albany, NY: SUNY Press.

Flax, J. (1990) *Thinking fragments: psychoanalysis, feminism and postmodernism in the contemporary West*. Berkeley, CA: University of California Press.

Folbre, N. (1994) *Who pays for the kids? Gender and the structures of constraints*. London: Routledge.

Foucault, M. (1988) *The history of sexuality (Vol. 3)*. New York: Vintage.

Fox Keller, E. (1985) *Reflections on gender and science*. London: Yale University Press.

Friedman, M. (Ed.) (1993) *What are friends for? Feminist perspectives on personal relationships and moral theory*. Ithaca, NY: Cornell University Press.

Froggett, L. (2002) *Love, hate and welfare: psychosocial approaches to policy and practice*. Bristol: Policy Press.

Frosh, S. (1991) *Identity crisis: modernity, psychoanalysis and the self*. London: Macmillan.

Gadow, S. (1990) The advocacy covenant: care as clinical subjectivity. In J. Stevenson and T. Tripp-Reimer (Eds), *Knowledge about care and caring* (pp. 33–40). Kansas City, MI: American Academy of Nursing.

Gardiner, J. (1997) *Gender, care and economics*. Basingstoke, UK: Macmillan.

Gilligan, C. (1982) *In a different voice: psychological theory and women's development*. Cambridge, MA: Harvard University Press.

Gilligan, C. (1991) Reframing resistance. In C. Gilligan, A. Rogers and D. Tolman (Eds), *Women, girls and psychotherapy* (pp. 5–31). New York: Haworth Press. Also in a special issue of *Women and Therapy*, 11(3/4).

Gilligan, C. (1993) Letter to readers, 1993. New preface to *In a different voice, (2nd edn)*. Cambridge, MA: Harvard University Press.

Gilligan, C. (2002) *The birth of pleasure*. New York: Alfred A Knopf.

Gilligan, C., Ward, J. and Taylor, J. (Eds) (1988) *Mapping the moral domain*. Cambridge, MA: Harvard University Press.

Groenhout, R. (1998) 'The virtue of care: Aristotelian ethics and contemporary ethics of care. In C. Freeland (Ed.), *Feminist interpretations of Aristotle*. University Park, PA: Penn State Press.

Hekman, S. (1999) *The future of differences: truth and method in feminist theory*. Cambridge: Polity Press.

Henriques, J., Hollway, W., Urwin, C., Venn, C. and. Walkerdine, V. (1984) *Changing the subject*. London: Methuen.

Hinshelwood, R.D. (1991) *Dictionary of Kleinian thought*. London: Free Association Books.

Hoagland, S. (1991) Some thoughts about caring. In C. Card (Ed.), *Feminist Ethics* (pp. 246–263). Lawrence, KA: University Press of Kansas.

Hogan, L. and Roseneil, S. (Eds) (2003) Special issue. *Feminist Theory*, 4,2.

Hoggett, P. (2000) *Emotional life and the politics of welfare*. Basingstoke: Macmillan.

Hollway, W. (2000) *Objectivity in British psychoanalysis*. Bolton College day conference 'Psychoanalysis and Society'. January, 2000.

Horney, K. (1926) The flight from womanhood: the masculinity complex in women. *International Journal of Psychoanaysis*, 7, 324–399.

Horney, K. (1932) The dread of woman. *International Journal of Psychoanaysis*, 13, 348–360.

Ignatieff, M. (1984) *The needs of strangers*. London: Hogarth Press.

Jordan, J. (1997) Clarity in connection: empathic knowing, desire and sexuality. In J. Jordan (Ed.), *Women's growth in diversity* (pp. 50–73). New York: Guilford Press.

Jordan, J., Kaplan, A., Miller, J., Stiver, I. and Surrey, J. (Eds) (1991) *Women's growth in connection*. New York: Guilford Press.

Kaplan, E.A. (1992) *Motherhood and representation: the mother in popular culture and melodrama*. London: Routledge.

Khan, M. (1975) Introduction. In Winnicott, D.W. *Collected papers. Through paediatrics to psycho-analysis*. London: Hogarth Press and Institute of Psychoanalysis.

Kitwood, T. (1990) *Concern for others: a new psychology of conscience and morality*. London: Routledge.

Klein, M. (1948) On the theory of anxiety and guilt. Reproduced in Klein, M. (Ed., 1988) *Envy and gratitude and other works 1946–1963* (pp. 25–42). London: Virago.

Klein, M. (1959) Our adult world and its roots in infancy. Reproduced in Klein, M. (Ed., 1988) *Envy and gratitude and other works 1946–1963* (pp. 247–263). London: Virago.

Klein, M. (1988) *Envy and gratitude and other works 1946–1963*. London: Virago.

Kohlberg, L. (1976) Moral stages and moralization: the cognitive–developmental approach. In T. Lickona (Ed.), *Moral development and behavior: theory, research and social issues*. New York: Holt Reinhart and Winston.

Kraemer, S. (1996) 'Betwixt the dark and the daylight' of maternal subjectivity: meditations on the threshold. *Psychoanalytic Dialogues*, 6, 765–791.

Larabee, M. (Ed.) (1993) *An ethic of care*. New York: Routledge.

Layton, L. (2004) Relational no more. In J.A. Winer, J.W. Anderson and C.C. Kieffer (Eds), *The annual of psychoanalysis, Vol. XXXII: Psychoanalysis and women*. Hillsdale, NJ: The Analytic Press.

Levinas, E. (1961) [1969 in translation] *Totality and infinity: essays in exteriority*. Pittsburgh, PA: Duquesne University Press.

Levinas, E. (1974) [1981 in translation] *Otherwise than being, or beyond essence*. New York: Springer

Levinas, E. (1999) [English translation] *Alterity and transcendence*. New York: Columbia University Press. (Original published 1985).

Loewald, H. (1980) *Papers in psychoanalysis*. New Haven, CT: Yale University Press.

McDougall, J. (1993) The dead father: on early psychic trauma and its relations to disturbance in sexual identity and creative activity. In D. Breen (Ed.), *The gender conundrum* (pp. 233–257). London: Routledge.

MacKenzie, C. and Stoljar, N. (Eds) (2000) *Relational autonomy: feminist perspectives on autonomy, agency and the social self*. New York: Oxford University Press.

Maguire, M. (1995) *Men, women, passion and power: gender issues in psychotherapy*. London: Routledge.

Mahler, M. (1968) *On human symbiosis and the vicissitudes of individuation*. New York: International Universities Press.

Main, M. (1993) Discourse, prediction, and recent studies in attachment: Implications for psychoanalysis. *Journal of the American Psychoanalytic Association*, 41, 209–244.

Marks, M. (2002) Letting fathers in. In J. Trowell and A. Etchegoyen (Eds), *The importance of fathers, a psychoanalytic re-evaluation* (pp. 93–106). Sussex: Brunner-Routledge.

Maynes, J. and Best, P. (1997) In the company of women: experiences of working with the lost mother. In W. Hollway and B. Featherstone (Eds), *Mothering and ambivalence* (pp. 119–135). London: Routledge.

Menzies, I. (1960) A case study in the functioning of social systems as a defence against anxiety. *Human Relations*, 13, 95–121.

Minsky, R. (1998) *Psychoanalysis and culture*. Cambridge: Polity Press.

Mitchell, J. (2000) *Mad men and medusas: reclaiming hysteria and the effects of sibling relationships on the human condition*. London: Penguin.

Mitchell, J. (2003) *Siblings: sex and violence*. Cambridge: Polity Press.

Mitchell, S. (2000) *Relationality: from attachment to intersubjectivity*. Hillsdale, NJ: The Analytic Press.

Monk, L. (1989) *Photographs that changed the world: the camera as witness, the photograph as evidence*. New York, Doubleday.

Mouffe, C. (2000) *The democratic paradox*. London: Verso.

Ogden, T. (1994) *Subject of analysis*. London: Karnac Books.

Ogden, T. (1994/1999) The analytic third. In S. Mitchell and L. Aron (Eds) (1999) *Relational psychoanalysis: the emergence of a tradition*. Hillsdale, NJ: The Analytic Press.

Ogden, T. (2001) *Conversations at the frontier of dreaming*. Northvale, NJ: Jason Aronson.

Parker, R. (1995) *Torn in two: The experience of maternal ambivalence*. London: Virago.

Parker, R. (1997) The production and purposes of maternal ambivalence. In W. Hollway and B. Featherstone (Eds), *Mothering and ambivalence* (pp. 17–36). London: Routledge.

Phillips, A. (1988) *Winnicott*. London: Fontana.

Phillips, L.M. (2000) *Flirting with danger: young women's reflections on sexuality and domination*. New York: New York University Press.

Piontelli, A. (1992) *From foetus to child: an observational and psychoanalytic study*. London: Routledge/Tavistock.

Pogge, T. (2002) *World poverty and human rights*. Cambridge: Polity Press.

Rabinow, P. (Ed.) (2000) *Michel Foucault: essential works 1954–1984. Vol. one: ethics*. London: Penguin.

Raphael-Leff, J. (1993) *Pregnancy: the inside story*. London: Sheldon Press.

Raphael-Leff, J. (Ed) (2003) *Parent-infant psychodynamics: Wild things, mirrors and ghosts*. London; Philadelphia: Wurr.

Rayner, E. (1990) *The independent mind in British psychoanalysis*. London: Free Assocation Books.

Risman, B.J. (1987) Intimate relationships from a microstructural perspective: men who mother. *Gender and Society*, 1, 6–32.

Robertson, J. and Robertson, J. (1989) *Separation and the very young*. London: Free Association Books.

Rose, G. (2006) Envisioning demands: photographs, families and strangers. In C. Barnett, J. Robinson and G. Rose (Eds), *A demanding world, DD205 Course Book* (pp. 189–236). The Open University: Milton Keynes.

Roseneil, S. (2000) *Common women, uncommon practices: the queer feminisms of Greenham*. London: Cassell.

Roseneil, S. (2004) Why we should care about friends: an argument for queering the care imaginary in social policy. *Social Policy and Society*, 3(4), 409–419.

Roseneil, S. (2007 unpublished) Sociability, sexuality, self: relationality and individualization.

Roseneil, R. and Hogan, L. (Eds) (2001) *Feminist theory*, 2,2. Special issue Gendering Ethics/The Ethics of Gender. London: Sage Publications.

Ruddick, S. (1980) Maternal Thinking. *Feminist Studies*, 6(2), 342–367.

Ruddick, S. (1989) *Maternal thinking: towards a politics of peace*. Boston MA: Beacon Press.

Rustin, M.J. (1991) *The good society and the inner world*. London: Verso.

Rycroft, C. (1972) *A critical dictionary of psychoanalysis*. London: Penguin.

Sampson, E.E. (2003) Unconditional kindness to strangers: Human sociality and the foundation for an ethical psychology. *Theory and Psychology*, 13(2), 147–175.

Scharff, D.E. (1992) *Refinding the object and reclaiming the self*. Northvale, NJ: Jason Aronson.

Segal, H. (1979) *Klein*. Glasgow: Fontana/Collins.

Sevenhuijsen, S. (1998) *Citizenship and the ethics of care*. London: Routledge.

Sevenhuijsen, S. (2002) *Steps towards an ethics of attention*. Paper presented at the 'Gender, sexuality and law' conference. Keele University, UK. 28–30 June 2002.

Sevenhuijsen, S. (2003) *Trace: a method for normative policy analysis from the ethic of care*. Paper presented to the Centre for Women's and Gender Research, University of Bergen, Norway, November 2003.

Silva, E.B. (1996) The transformation of mothering. In E.B. Silva (Ed.), *Good enough mothering. Feminist perspectives on lone motherhood* (pp. 10–35), London: Routledge.

Skeggs, B. (1997) *Formations of class and gender*. London: Sage.

Smart, C., Neale, B. and Wade, A. (2001) *The changing experience of childhood*. Cambridge: Polity Press.

Sullivan, A. (1998) *Love undetectable: reflections on friendship, sex and survival*. London: Chatto and Windus.

Surrey, J. (1991) The 'self-in-relation': a theory of women's development. In J. Jordan, A. Kaplan, J. Miller, I. Stiver and J. Surrey (Eds), *Women's growth in connection* (pp. 53–66). New York: Guilford Press.

Target, M. and Fonagy, P. (2002) Fathers in modern psychoanalysis and in society: the role of the father and child development. In J. Trowell and A. Etchegoyen (Eds), *The importance of fathers, a psychoanalytic re-evaluation* (pp. 45–66). Sussex, UK: Brunner-Routledge.

Titmuss, R.M. (1970) *Gift relationship: from human blood to social policy.* London: Allen and Unwin.

Tronto, J. (1993) *Moral boundaries.* London: Routledge.

Turp, M. (2002) *Hidden self harm: narratives from psychotherapy.* London: Jessica Kingsley.

Turp, M. (2004) The capacity for self care. *Infant Observation*, 7,1, 108–126.

Tustin, F. (1986) *Autistic barriers in neurotic patients.* London: Karnac.

Waddell, M. (1998) *Inside lives.* London: Tavistock.

Waterman, B. (2003) *Birth of an adoptive, foster or stepmother: beyond biological mothering attachments.* London: Jessica Kingsley.

Williams, F. (2001) In and beyond New Labour: towards a new political ethic of care. *Critical Social Policy*, 21(4), 467–493.

Williams, F. (2004) *Rethinking families.* London: Calouste Gulbenkian Foundation.

Winnicott, D.W. (1958) *Collected papers. Through paediatrics to psychoanalysis.* New York: Basic Books

Winnicott, D.W. (1958) Mind and its relation to the psyche-soma. In Winnicott D.W. *Through paediatrics to psychoanalysis* (pp. 243–254). New York: Basic Books. (Original work published 1949)

Winnicott, D.W. (1960/1990) The theory of the parent-infant relationship. In D.W. Winnicott *The maturational process and the facilitating environment* (1965/1990) (pp. 37–55). London: Karnac and the Institute of Psychoanalysis.

Winnicott, D.W. (1965) *The maturational process and the facilitating environment.* London: Hogarth Press.

Winnicott, D.W. (1968) *Babies and their mothers.* London: Free Association Books.

Winnicott, D.W. (1971) Contemporary concepts of adolescent development and their implication for higher education. In D.W. Winnicott *Playing and reality* (1971/2005) (pp. 186–203). London: Routledge.

Winnicott, D.W. (1974) Fear of breakdown. *International Review of Psychoanalysis* 1,1, 103–107.

Winnicott, D.W. (1975a) *Collected papers. Through paediatrics to psychoanalysis.* London: Hogarth.

Winnicott, D. W. (1975b) Hate in the counter-transference. In Winnicott D.W. *Collected papers. Through paediatrics to psychoanalysis.* London: Hogarth. (Original work published 1947)

Winnicott, D.W. (1975c) The depressive position in relation to normal emotional development. In Winnicott, D.W. *Collected papers. Through paediatrics to psychoanalysis.* London: Hogarth Press. (Original work published 1954)

Winnicott, D.W. (1975d) Transitional objects and transitional phenomena. In Winnicott, D.W. *Collected papers. Through paediatrics to psychoanalysis.* London: Hogarth Press. (Original work published 1951)

Wolf, N. (2001) *Misconceptions: truth, lies and the unexpected journey to motherhood.* London: Chatto and Windus.

INDEX

146